The Mysterie

The
Mysteries of March

Hans Urs von Balthasar on
the Incarnation and Easter

by

John Saward

Foreword by Rowan Williams

COLLINS

Collins Religious Publishing
8 Grafton Street, London W1X 3LA

Collins Dove
PO Private Bag 200
Burwood, Victoria 3125

Collins New Zealand
PO Box 1
Auckland

© 1990 John Saward
First published 1990
ISBN 0 00 599198 6

Typographical design by Ann Hewitt
Typesetting by K.G. Farren, Mill Street, Scarborough
Made and printed in Great Britain by William Collins Sons Ltd,
Glasgow

CONTENTS

FOREWORD

British readers are proverbially nervous about philosophical or religious writers with German names, and a name that appears on the spine of a massive rank of plump volumes, mostly in brown and grey covers, does nothing to take away their apprehensiveness. John Saward's remarkable little book should persuade even the most wary that Hans Urs von Balthasar, for all that his output is large and often difficult, is not a name to fear. This is a book about theology, Christian reflection, as celebration and thanksgiving, because that is the motive power behind Balthasar's work. It is, like that work, an invitation into the imaginative and spiritual richness of the Catholic Christian tradition, and a reminder that, as Balthasar so clearly understood, the life of the spirit dries up when the imagination is not allowed to feed on the fullness of doctrine, liturgy and scripture.

Balthasar is, in one way, a resolutely "unmodern" writer, sitting quite light to critical approaches to the Bible, for instance, and seeing with a clinical eye how European rationality from the seventeenth century onwards has more and more tied itself into destructive patterns of self-obsession, alienated from the concrete challenge of the "otherness" of history, art, community and the body itself. Like other contemporary thinkers, he identifies the intellectual "modernity" of Europe as a sickness of the spirit. For all its liberating achievements, it has been drawn inexorably into a realm where human beings are understood as bundles of material requirements, competing with each other for feeding space, and so are trapped in the melodramas of their private needs; a realm in which threats and the passion for security dominate; a realm which we can easily recognize as the social and political world of the late twentieth century.

The good news for such a world cannot lie in generalized optimism about the spiritual capacities of human beings. For Balthasar, it lies only in the achieved fact of Jesus Christ. "It depends on him", he has written, "whether we can dare to address being as love, and thus all beings as worthy of love". And the good news is not a theory or a programme, but the possibility of belonging *with* Jesus *in* the community of the Church. Jesus in the gospels is in an important sense a solitary and unique figure, but he is not a lonely romantic hero: his mission is realized in and through the varied responses of those around him, the total self-gift of Mary, the turbulent and ambiguous service of Peter's leadership in the community, the contemplative faithfulness of John, the prophetic protest of Paul. Understanding Jesus and the Church of Jesus is understanding how we find our calling in and with these figures. We have a dangerously narrow and distorted view of the Church if we fail to see the essential interlocking of our vocations in the pattern established in these New Testament models and symbols. Balthasar's vision of the Church as bearer of good news involves a vision of the universal, central calling of Christians to the sheer empty availability of Mary (not passive but supremely active, because giving in love is the most demanding of all acts); of the necessary stresses, conflicts and compromises of institutional life, summed up in the Petrine office; of the hidden life of the community as the forming of love and wisdom among human beings; and of the boundary-breaking pressures of mission. Catholic Christianity, for Balthasar, shows the fullness of Christ, because in it all these vocations are given space and woven together.

Is Balthasar a writer who simply presents a superbly integrated pattern of Christian symbols, rich and satisfying, but offering no point of entry to the contemporary secular mentality? He may sometimes seem so to the hasty reader. But if Balthasar is unmodern in many respects, it is equally true that few theologians can match his knowledge and penetration of modern European intellectual and cultural life. At moment after moment in his writing, some point from the Christian tradition is set alongside some element in the cultural history of Europe, past or present, to challenge or illuminate. He does not seek to study the contemporary world in the hope that, at the end of the day, some version of residual Christianity can be produced from it, like a rabbit from a hat; rather he reads his way deeply into Christian history in its own right and cultural history in its own right, in the conviction that the quest and energy animating the latter must finally be capable of being "brought home" in terms of the Christian revelation, and its true direction and desire laid open. So he is never a conventional apologist; he is more interested in uncovering the kind of analogy or juxtaposition of Christian and non-Christian worlds that can fuse both in a transfiguring perception – a perception of the God who is able to be present, to be real, in all those places where he seems most signally absent. Such is the God who is with us as Jesus, crucified and descending into Hell.

John Saward has performed a vastly impressive feat of synthesis and compression, without ever resorting to mechanical summary and repetitive cataloguing of ideas. With a distinctive stylistic richness of his own, he has thought and imagined his way into the heart of Balthasar's theological world and given us a meditation on the mysteries of the Word made flesh that is both an introduction to a great mind and something more. He does not gloss over aspects of Balthasar's scheme that may be difficult or uncongenial, or simply (as with Balthasar's use of the visionary insights of Adrienne von Speyr) bafflingly unfamiliar to the theological mindset of the English-speaking world. He is not afraid either to challenge Balthasar on some matters, or to speak in his own right as a theologian. This will not be an uncontroversial book to read, even for the most sympathetic; many – like the writer of this Foreword – will have questions and disagreements here and there. But the last thing we should ask of a good book (let alone a good book about God) is that it be bland. Better to ask it to be demanding, enriching and productive of gratitude – to the writer, to his subject, to God. Anyone asking this will not be disappointed in these pages.

ROWAN WILLIAMS
Oxford, Octave of the
Transfiguration 1989

PREFACE

It is hard to think of a more *grateful* theologian than Hans Urs von Balthasar. "Everyone owes himself", he once wrote, "not only to God, but to the whole Church". Not only in expressly autobiographical pieces but throughout his works, he never failed to acknowledge his debt to other people: to the saints of the past in Heaven, but also to his family and the friends he made on earth. It is right, therefore, to preface this study of his theology with gratitude – first of all to Father Balthasar himself, for what he has done for the whole Church as her greatest theologian of this century, and for what he did for me, as for countless other individuals, by his spiritual counsel and great kindness. What follows is dedicated to his memory. Secondly, I must thank Father John Osman, Catholic Chaplain to the University of Cambridge, for the invitation to give the 1989 Fisher Lectures, from which this book developed, and for his warm hospitality. Then there are the friends, old and new, from whom I have learnt so much, and without whose encouragement and prayers *The Mysteries of March* would never have been written: Father John Butters, Stratford and Léonie Caldecott, Richard and Carol Downer, Father Kevin Gallagher, Peter McDonald and all the members of "our own dear CRUX", Canon John McHugh, Monsignor Lawrence McReavy, Monsignor Richard Malone, John and Frances Morrill, Father Aidan Nichols OP, Father Robert Ombres OP, Father Dermot Power, Father Charles Smith, and Professor Rowan Williams. Finally, there is an old friend who is somehow always new: this book is for her, and for our daughters.

John Saward
Ushaw College, Durham
Holy Saturday
25 March 1989

HANS URS VON BALTHASAR
A BIOGRAPHICAL NOTE

12 August 1905	Born in Lucerne, Switzerland. Educated by the Benedictines at Engelberg and the Jesuits at Feldkirch. Studied *Germanistik* and Philosophy at the Universities of Vienna, Berlin, and Zurich.
1925	First article published on "The Development of the Musical Idea".
27 October 1928	Awarded a doctorate for his dissertation on "The History of the Eschatological Problem in Modern German Literature".
31 October 1929	Entered the Society of Jesus.
1929–1931	Novitiate at Feldkirch.
1931–1933	Philosophy at the Berchmanskolleg in Pullach near Munich. Contact with *Erich Przywara*.
1933–1937	Theology at Lyons (Fourvière). Contact with *Henri de Lubac*.
26 July 1939	Ordained to the priesthood.
1937–1939	Associate editor of the journal *Stimmen der Zeit* in Munich. Cooperation with *Hugo and Karl Rahner*.
Late 1939	Tertianship (concluding phase of Jesuit formation) in Pullach.

1940–1948	University chaplain at Basel. Dialogue with *Karl Barth*.
1 November 1940	Received *Adrienne von Speyr* (+ 1967), a married laywoman and doctor, into the Catholic Church. With her eventually founded a secular institute, the Community of St John.
1950	Left the Society of Jesus. Incardinated as a secular priest in the Swiss diocese of Chur.
1950–1988	Active in Basel as leader of the Community of St John, publisher, and theological writer.
1969	Appointed by Pope Paul VI to International Theological Commission.
1972	Founded with others *Communio: International Catholic Review*.
1984	Presented with the Pope Paul VI International Prize by Pope John Paul II.
22 May 1987	Awarded the Wolfgang Amadeus Mozart Prize in Innsbrück.
29 May 1988	Nominated as a Cardinal by Pope John Paul II.
26 June 1988	Died suddenly in Basel.

INTRODUCTION

There are years when, by date, the Annunciation falls during Holy Week, even on Easter Sunday; in 1989, for example, the twenty-fifth of March was Holy Saturday. In the Latin Church the problem of such double booking is solved by transferring the feast to a day outside the privileged Paschal period. However, in the Churches of the Byzantine rite, the solemnity of the Incarnation stands its ground alongside the commemoration of the Lord's Passion and Resurrection. If the Annunciation coincides with "Great Friday" or "Great Saturday", these cease to be the two days of the year when the Eucharist is not celebrated; the divine liturgy is served in honour of the Incarnation, and there is a hectic duplication of offices. This custom may look like just another example of oriental delight in complication, but it is much more than that. First, it reflects a tradition going back at least as far as Tertullian, according to which Our Lord died on the Cross on the eighth day before the Calends of April, that is to say, the twenty-fifth of March, the very day on which, by a later reckoning, he had been conceived by the Holy Spirit in the womb of the Virgin.[1] Secondly, both the eastern liturgical practice and the calendrical tradition upon which it is based express an intuition of faith, the Church's sense that the "mysteries of March" – the Incarnation, the Cross, and the Resurrection – are inseparably connected. Christian poets have always loved to entwine them. For example, St Ephrem, the fourth century Syriac writer, speaks of the new and everlasting springtime inaugurated by the coincidences of the month to which he gives the Semitic name of "Nisan".

> In the month of Nisan, when the seed sprouts in the warm air, the Sheaf sowed itself in the earth. Death reaped and swallowed it up in Sheol, but the medicine of life, hidden within, burst Sheol open. In Nisan, when lambs bleat in the meadow, the Paschal Lamb entered His Mother's womb.[2]

In 1608 the Annunciation fell on Good Friday and in England inspired one of John Donne's finest *Divine Poems*. Donne looks at the Virgin Mother, "Reclus'd at home, Publique at Golgotha", and considers the strange simultaneity of conception and crucifixion.

> At once a Sonne is promis'd her, He her to John;
> Not fully a mother, Shee's in Orbitie,
> At once receiver and the legacie.
> All this, and all betweene, this day hath showne,
> Th'Abridgement of Christ's story, which makes one
> (As in plaine Maps, the furthest West is East)
> Of the Angel's *Ave* and *Consummatum est*.[3]

Interweaving the mysteries is not just the business of poets; according to the First Vatican Council, it is the proper task of theologians. We attain a deeper understanding of divine revelation when we come to see how all its mysteries fit together as a true and splendid whole.[4] The very word "Catholic" implies wholeness and therefore interconnection.[5] In one of his *Catechetical Lectures*, the fourth century Church Father, St Cyril of Jerusalem, says that the Church is Catholic not just because she is geographically and socially universal, but because she "teaches universally and completely all the dogmas which ought to come to men's knowledge".[6] For the Fathers, the Catholic faith is the full faith, whereas heresy is the diminishing of the fullness, the selection (*hairesis*) of a part to the neglect of the whole.[7]

In our own time no theologian has more beautifully demonstrated the interlocking wholeness of Catholic Christianity than Hans Urs von Balthasar, who died on 26 June 1988, two days before he was to be made a Cardinal by the Pope.[8] If the faith is a whole, he argues, then theology, the understanding of the faith, must be holistic too.

> Theology can only perform its task by circular repetitions of that which is ever-greater. Parcelling it out in isolated individual tracts is its certain death.[9]

In other words, theology must connect not divide.

> No Christology without the doctrine of the Trinity (and, of course, *vice versa*), no Christology, for that matter, without the fulfilment of the Old Testament tradition and the missionary opening up of the Church to the whole world . . . The doctrine of redemption presupposes a Christology (in turn implying the Trinity of God) . . . What is more, the soteriology which speaks of Christ "assuming what is ours" contains within it the doctrine of the Eucharist, in which he gives himself to us and we receive what is his.[10]

The Catholic unity of the faith, which theology tries to reflect, is not man-made. It has its source, according to Balthasar, in the Trinity revealed in Christ. As the threefold structure of the Creed shows, what unites the dogmas of the faith is their common reference, through Christ, to the Triune God.

There can be no question, then, according to Balthasar, of an ecumenical core of "essential Christianity", to which Catholicism adds its "optional extras" (Mary, the Petrine Office, and so on). The truth is the God-given whole; the doctrines of the denominations are so many subtractions from the catholicity of revelation. True, there may be times when certain parts of the whole are more evidently valued among non-Catholic Christians than by Catholics. Yet it is to the Catholic Church alone that the splendid ensemble of revealed truth has been entrusted by her divine Founder.[11] So Mary and Peter can never be regarded as "supplementary figures". They belong to what Balthasar calls the "Christological constellation"; without them there is only an abstract Christ and a formless Church.[12]

The division to whose healing Balthasar has most ardently devoted himself is the tragic divorce between theology and holiness. In his own career the unity of *sacra doctrina* and *vita sancta* has taken a particularly poignant form. He has on many occasions insisted that his theological work is inseparable from the life and writings of a married laywoman, the Swiss mystic Adrienne von Speyr, whom he received into the Catholic Church in 1940, and whose spiritual director he remained until her death in 1967. He received, he said, more theologically from her than she did from him.[13] The extraordinary graces she received furnished him with many, if not most, of the distinctive insights of his mature theology. This is particularly true of his theology of the Easter Triduum, for each Holy Week Adrienne was given the grace to share mystically in Christ's Passion and Descent into Hell, an experience which gave a wholly new direction to his work.[14]

The wholeness or catholicity of divine revelation is best understood when we see it, as Balthasar does in his *Theological Aesthetic*, as *Gestalt*, form or figure, a term with echoes of Goethe as well as of Aristotle, Albert, and Thomas.[15] A *Gestalt* is something concrete and objective, with a unity that is more than just the sum of its parts. Applied christologically, it signifies the incarnate form, the real flesh and blood figure, of Jesus as expressing the inexhaustible glory of God's Triune love.[16] To appreciate a beautiful form, you have to see it as a whole and from every angle, or, in the case of musical beauty, you have to hear it with all its harmonies. There is always something new to see or hear, and yet still it is the same thing, beauty ever ancient, ever new. Now the form of revelation is not a lifeless statue but a dramatic love that wants to give itself.[17] And so when the believer, in and with the Church, contemplates it, he cannot be just a neutral observer. The prodigality with which the Son of God loves me and gives himself up for me seizes me, sweeps me off my feet. To perceive the splendour of the Trinity's self-giving love in Christ is, therefore, to be enraptured and engaged.[18] It means letting oneself, like Mary, be caught up by the Spirit into the incarnate Son's ecstatic and Eucharistic self-surrender to the Father. The *Theological Aesthetic* leads directly, therefore, to the second and third parts of Balthasar's trilogy: the *Theodramatic* and *Theologic*.[19] When God reveals himself in his Son, he shows forth his glory, dramatically pours out his goodness, and definitively utters his Word of truth.[20]

The philosophy and theology of *Gestalt* proves that Balthasar's "sense of the whole" is not a vague syncretism. The universal, for him, is always rooted in the concrete. The incarnate Word is, in his very person, the *universale concretum et personale*, God's universal truth and love in concrete form.[21] The fullness of the faith reflects the Trinitarian plenitude of God, but our

xix

only access to that plenitude is through the Virgin-born, crucified and risen flesh of the Son; as St Paul says, the *plerôma* of the Godhead dwells in Christ corporeally (Col. 2:9).[22] The Father's eternal Son, in whom all creation is to be recapitulated (cf. Eph.3:10), did not assume some Platonic idea of general manhood, but a complete and concrete human nature. The Universal Redeemer is Jesus of Nazareth, born of the Virgin Mary, crucified under Pontius Pilate, raised up in his human body on the third day. And his Church, the inclusive ark of salvation, is built, not in the air, but on the visible rock that is Peter.[23]

The range of Balthasar's knowledge – of literature and philosophy (both ancient and modern), of the Fathers and Scholastics, of all the great theologians and spiritual writers of the Church – is unrivalled. His mentor, Henri Cardinal de Lubac, once described him as "the most cultured man of our times".[24] It is important to see the breadth of his reading and writing as the practical application of that principle of catholicity or concrete universality which governs all his thinking. Catholic Christianity, in its very unique-ness and incomparable greatness, can incorporate all the truth of the world. Truth, he says, is symphonic, neither bland unison nor harsh cacophony, but a gloriously dramatic polyphony.[25] And so he wants to attune his ear to the tradition's full harmonies – the New Testament with the Old Testament, the Greek Fathers as well as the Latin, Bonaventure alongside Thomas, the "lay style" of a Dante or Péguy to match the "clerical style" of an Augustine or Anselm.[26]

It is with the help of this witness to faith's fullness that I am going to try in this book to explore what links the mysteries of March: the Annunciation with the Paschal Triduum; Nazareth with Calvary, Sheol, and the empty tomb; the Incarnation of God the Son with his Passion, Death, and Resurrection. My subject is not Balthasar himself, but the very heart of Christianity as opened up by him. I want to draw on his insights, not slavishly or uncritically, and yet with gratitude and respect. I want to place them in the context of the great tradition of the Church, which he understood so well and treasured so intensely.[27]

One

The Incarnation and the Cross

1
LADY DAY AND GOOD FRIDAY

The Annunciation – "Lady Day", to use its old
English name – is the feast of the Incarnation. The
Word was made flesh in Nazareth when the Blessed
Virgin Mary said to the angel Gabriel, "Be it done
unto me according to thy word" (Luke 1:38). It was
exactly then that, by the overshadowing of the Holy
Spirit, a body was fashioned from the Virgin's flesh
and blood, a rational soul was created and infused
into the body, and, in the same instant, the complete
human nature was united to the divine person of the
Father's eternal Son.[1] God became a human being at
the moment of his conception in the Virgin's womb.
The question I want to ask is this: how does the
Incarnation, celebrated on the Solemnity of the
Annunciation, relate to the other great mystery of
March, the Cross? Balthasar considers this question in
detail in two of his most important works: *Mysterium
Paschale*, his contribution to the encyclopedic *Myster-
ium Salutis*, and the New Testament volume of *Herr-
lichkeit*. His answer in both is the same: "To say
Incarnation is to say Cross".[2]

> There is probably no theological proposition where
> the East is so much at one with the West as that
> which says that the Incarnation happens for the
> sake of the redemption of mankind on the Cross
> . . . "Assuming human nature" means taking over

3

man's concrete destiny with suffering, death, Hell, in solidarity with all men.[3]

Balthasar cites a large number of Patristic texts, both Greek and Latin, to prove his thesis. I shall give just two, one from each tradition. First, St Athanasius:

The impassible Logos assumes a body . . . in order to take upon himself what is ours and to offer it in sacrifice . . . so that the whole man might obtain salvation.

Secondly, Pope St Leo the Great:

He descended into what is ours (*in nostra*) to assume not just the substance but also the condition of sinful nature.[4]

In Balthasar's opinion, these texts give the lie to a "widespread myth" in the textbooks that, for the Greek Fathers, the redemption is accomplished by the act of the Incarnation alone. No, "the final goal of the Incarnation is the Cross".[5]

Without ceasing to be impassible and immortal in his divine nature, the eternal Son assumes on Lady Day a passible and mortal human nature, so that on Good Friday he may truly suffer and die in that human nature for our redemption. God the Son not only makes his own our human nature in its entirety, material body and rational soul (what St Leo calls our "substance", "what is ours"), he also assumes it in its concrete "condition". This is what St Paul means when he says that the Son "takes the form of a servant" (Phil. 2:7) and is sent "in the likeness of sinful flesh" (Rom. 8:3). He took our humanity in its slavish state of possibility and mortality, with its hellish destiny of Godforsakenness, though without sin. Freely, out of love for mankind, he chose to share the

4

lot of fallen man, to identify himself with us in our "being towards death" (*Dasein zum Tode*).[6]

Balthasar's view of the connection between the Incarnation and the Cross sheds light on the centuries-old debate among western theologians about the motive of the Incarnation. The issue, at least as it is presented in the textbooks, is as follows. The Scotists (those who follow Duns Scotus) argue that the Incarnation was willed unconditionally for its own sake, so that, even in an unfallen world, the Son would have become man to glorify the Father by recapitulating all creation in himself (cf. Eph. 1:10). By contrast, the Thomists (those who follow St Thomas Aquinas) maintain that the Incarnation depends, in some way, on the "happy fault", the "necessary sin of Adam", so that, in an unfallen world, the Son would not have become man. Balthasar does not take sides in this controversy. First, with his profound knowledge of the tradition, he is aware that the thinking of the two great Scholastics themselves is more balanced and accommodating of other insights than the often rigid positions of their successors.[7] Secondly, he refuses to speculate about hypotheticals. His theology is concrete, concerned with realities not possibilities. Its primary object is "the very concrete personal reality of the God-Man who suffers, descends to Hell, and rises again 'for me', 'for us'".[8] True, as much as any Scotist, he wants to affirm that God became man to redeem us not only *from* but *for* something: entry, by grace, into the life of the Blessed Trinity.

> Christ came as the Redeemer of mankind, but in no sense did he obtain for us a mere discount in guilt, but rather the fulness of all divine gifts – summed up in the phrase "adoption as God's children", which the Father bestows on us as, so to

speak, a matter of course when he gives up his only Son for us.[9]

However, he is disquieted by the ease with which Scotism lends itself to exploitation by the "evolutionary" christologies of modern times (for example, those of Teilhard de Chardin and Karl Rahner), which diminish the gratuitousness of the Incarnation, making it look like the inevitable outcome of a cosmic process.

In *Mysterium Paschale*, Balthasar argues that the best insights of both Thomist and Scotist schools can be reconciled, without facile harmonization, when we acknowledge that by serving his creatures and washing their feet, God reveals himself at his most truly divine and shows his supreme glory.[10] We do not have to choose between the "Scotist" emphasis on the Son coming to glorify the Father and crown creation, and the "Thomist" emphasis on the Son coming to redeem mankind by his Passion. With St John the Evangelist, Balthasar sees that it is precisely in the hour of his humiliation and obedience unto death that the Redeemer-Son draws all creation to himself (cf. John 12:32) and glorifies his Father (cf. 17:1ff). His ear is attuned to the "symphony" of revelation, to its richly chromatic chords, which contain in perfect harmony the notes dear to Thomist and Scotist alike. He thereby aligns himself with the simple believer, whose childlike "sense of the faith" cuts through the disputes of the learned and reaches the heart of the mystery.

2
THE INCARNATION, THE CROSS, AND THE TRINITY

The Revelation of the Trinity

The mysteries of March are manifestations of the Trinity. The Annunciation is the first of these. "The Son of the Father allows himself to be borne into a human womb, and so the heavens open in a new way and reveal a threefold life in God."[1] In writing this, perhaps Balthasar has in mind the lovely Annunciations of medieval art, where the Dove is depicted carrying a cross-bearing infant Son from the heavenly Father to the Virgin's womb.[2] It is only to the Second Person of the Trinity, God the Son, that human nature is united, yet the whole Trinity is at work in the uniting. The Father sends the Son; the Son lets himself be sent; and the overshadowing Spirit fashions a body for him from the flesh of the assenting Virgin. As St John of the Cross says in one of his romances, summarizing the teaching of St Thomas and the Fathers before him:

> Though the three Persons worked the wonder,
> It only happened in the One,
> So was the Word made incarnation
>   In Mary's womb, a Son.[3]

This is the first act of Trinitarian revelation. Its climax is the Easter Mystery, the Passover of the Son: his

7

Cross, Resurrection, and sending of the Spirit from the Father. Balthasar's theology circles round the Johannine paradox that the glory of God's Triune love is supremely manifested in the human form of the Son broken and obedient unto death.[4] And he sees the Resurrection, too, as a Trinitarian event: "the Father . . . awakens the Son from the dead so that He, as one freshly united with the Father can send forth God's Spirit into the Church".[5]

Balthasar tries to connect, without confusing, what the Greek Fathers call "theology" and "economy", that is to say, the doctrine of the eternal, inner life of the Trinity, and the revelation of the Trinity, in and through Christ, in the economy of salvation. Modern theology makes more or less the same distinction when it speaks of the "immanent Trinity" and the "economic Trinity". Balthasar's strategy presupposes the teaching of the fifth ecumenical council (Constantinople II, 553) that the "one person, one hypostasis" in Christ, of which the Chalcedonian Definition speaks, is the Second Person of the Blessed Trinity, the pre-existent hypostasis of God the Son.[6] It is this Trinitarian person who in the womb of the Virgin assumes human nature and in that human nature suffers, dies, and rises again. Balthasar, therefore, insists on seeing the whole mystery of Christ in a Trinitarian light, for "as God, *and also as man*, he exists only in his relation to the Father in the unity of the Holy Spirit".[7]

The Son is *Trinitarian revelation*. He "produces on earth an extrapolation of the Trinity: he lives in a completely Trinitarian way, though he becomes a man among men" . . . "He lives in the Holy Spirit, whom he receives, and in the vision of the Father, with whom he speaks in prayer, and whose will He does".[8]

8

This real human being of flesh and blood, conceived and born of the Virgin Mary, crucified under Pontius Pilate, resurrected on the third day in his human body, is the Father's eternal Son made man and thus "the concretion of the Triune God".[9]

Karl Rahner has described Balthasar's interconnecting of Christology and Trinitarian doctrine as "Neo-Chalcedonian", the term used to describe the Greek theologians of the late fifth, sixth, and seventh centuries who, in clarifying and making precise the teaching of Chalcedon, defended the orthodoxy of the statement that "One of the Trinity suffered for us". Rahner would prefer to avoid this formula because of the risk it runs of confusing the two natures of Christ. By contrast, Balthasar, who has written a classic study of the greatest of the "Neo-Chalcedonians" (St Maximus the Confessor)[10], maintains the thesis that, without the "One of the Trinity" formula in its orthodox interpretation, there can be no theology of redemption.

> I cannot see how we can make anything of the *pro nobis* of Christ's Cross and Resurrection if the One Crucified and Risen is not "One of the Trinity". If he is not, then it may be true that "when it's going bad for me, I get nothing out of it going badly for God".[11]

It is because their subject is a divine person, One of the Trinity, that Christ's truly human sufferings have a universal inclusiveness and infinite saving power.[12] Because it is more precisely the Second Person, God the Son, who suffers as man in a filial way, in human obedience to his Father, we can see the whole drama of redemption as a revelation of the Trinity. This is the Neo-Chalcedonian Fathers' tremendous contribution to the tradition: their insistence that "the economy [of salvation] is the manifestation of a loving Triune God".[13]

The Economic and Immanent Trinity

"No Trinitarian doctrine without Christology", says Balthasar, "no Christology without Trinitarian doctrine". *No Trinitarian doctrine without Christology*: the doctrine of the Trinity is not the product of unaided reason; it has been revealed to us in and by the Word made flesh. "We only know Father, Son, and Holy Spirit as 'Divine Persons' through the figure of Jesus Christ and the way he relates [to the Father and the Spirit]".[14] But we must immediately add: *no Christology without Trinitarian doctrine*. Only if God, eternally and internally, is Father, Son, and Holy Spirit, can we understand the threefoldness of divine revelation. The drama of salvation history is made possible by the primordial interplay of God's interior life, the mutual love of Father and Son in the Holy Spirit.

God is Trinity, not just in revelation, but in himself, in his innermost being. Balthasar is, therefore, critical of the modern tendency to confuse the immanent with the economic Trinity, or even to dismiss the very notion of an immanent Trinity. Rahner's often quoted axiom – "The economic Trinity *is* the immanent Trinity, and *vice versa*" – he regards as dangerously ambiguous.[15] He is even more critical of the book by Jürgen Moltmann, *The Crucified God*, which makes the crucifixion a directly Trinitarian event. Behind this muddle, Balthasar sees the baleful influence of "Process Theology" and, beyond that, the spectre of Hegel.[16]

It is essential, says Balthasar, that we distinguish between the eternal processions within the Godhead and the process of saving history outside it. To confuse the two, to embroil the Triune Godhead directly in the happenings of the world, is to "turn him into a tragic, mythological god", who uses creation and the Cross to fulfil himself.[17] That is not the

God revealed in Jesus, the God who creates and redeems, not by any mechanical necessity, but out of generous love. What is more – and this is the central issue in the discussion of the economic and immanent Trinity – the God who shows such generous love towards us in creation and redemption is already love in himself, absolutely and eternally, as Trinity in Unity and Unity in Trinity. God does not "become" love when he creates the world as an "opposite number". He already is love in himself, Father and Son loving one another in the Holy Spirit, "above and beyond any world".[18]

> We need to find a way of seeing the immanent Trinity as the ground of the cosmic process (including the Cross), yet in such a way that it does not look like just a formal process of self-mediation (as it is with Rahner), nor as mixed up in the cosmic process (as it is with Moltmann). Instead, we have to think of the immanent Trinity as that eternal and absolute self-giving, so that God is seen as being in himself absolute love. This is the only thing that will explain his free self-giving to the world as love without God needing the cosmic process and the Cross to become (and "mediate") himself.[19]

The Passion of Jesus and the Impassibility of the Trinity

The most urgent question for anyone seeking to weave together "theology" and "economy" is the bearing of the Incarnation and Passion of the Son on the impassibility of the Triune Godhead, its incapacity for suffering. In defending the doctrine of the Incarnation in the culture of pagan Greece and Rome, the Church Fathers took care to distinguish it from the

11

mythological idea of a changeable, suffering god. The Incarnation, they never tire of repeating, is not the changing of God into a man but the taking up of manhood into God.[20] It is a becoming without change. St Cyril of Alexandria states the classical axiom: "immutable by nature as God, remaining what he always was, what he is, what he will always be, he became Son of Man".[21] Similarly, the Fathers teach that, though God the Son assumes a passible human nature, and in it really suffers for us, he remains absolutely impassible in his divine nature. As St Athanasius says, "the same person suffers and does not suffer", suffers as man, does not suffer as God.[22]

Balthasar's approach to the immutability and impassibility of God is subtle and nuanced. On the one hand, he stands with Patristic and Scholastic tradition in refusing to attribute change and suffering univocally to God.

> Any kind of "process theology", which identifies the cosmic process (together with God's involvement in it, including the Cross) with the eternal and timeless "process" of the hypostases in God, is strictly ruled out.[23]

On the other hand, he is critical of St Thomas' view that the hypostatic union, like every relation between the created and the Uncreated, exists really in the human nature but in God "only according to reason (*secundum rationem tantum*)".[24] Balthasar rejects "Patripassianism", any suggestion that the Father suffers in the same sense in which the Son does, but he adds, somewhat enigmatically, that "only a hair's breadth" separates the real suffering of the God-Man and the non-suffering of God.[25] He has little patience with the view of some modern theologians that God's impassibility is simply an ethical "attitude of covenant fidelity". No, says Balthasar, "the Bible . . . glimpses *through* his economic attitude an attribute of God as he is in himself".[26] He is unshakeably faithful to the covenant because he is, of his very nature, immovable. Nevertheless, says Balthasar, the post-Patristic period understands divine impassibility more narrowly than the Fathers themselves do. He would like to think, with Lactantius, that, while there can be no feelings in the Godhead, the divine "pity", "wrath" and "tenderness" of which Scripture speaks are more than anthropomorphisms: they are "forms of the divine vitality" which can be understood by "analogy with human emotions without drawing God into 'passibility'."[27]

While agreeing with the Scholastics that there can be no univocal change and suffering in God, Balthasar feels that their presentation of divine immutability fails to bring out the dynamism, the sheer eventfulness, of God's inner Trinitarian life. And so, though refusing to ascribe suffering to God as God, he says that we must be prepared to admit that there is something in him "which justifies not only the possibility and occurrence of all the world's pains but also, in addition, God's participation in them [as man], to the point of effectively, vicariously taking Godlessness on to himself".[28] The Son suffers as man, not as God, but there must be something in the Godhead, in the immanent Trinity, that makes possible and is expressed by that human suffering of a divine person.

Pursuing his inquiry along these lines, in the final volume of his *Theodramatik*, Balthasar expresses sympathy with the argument of Father Jean Galot SJ that the "renunciation" involved in the intra-Trinitarian ecstasy is the model and source of the renunciations implied by a love of mankind that is incarnate and crucified.[29] Balthasar makes use of this insight, though he is unhappy about Galot's distinction between the Trinity's untouchable inner life and its "affectively", if not "effectively" touchable relation to the world.[30] It is an idea developed by Jacques Maritain in one of his last published articles that Balthasar finds most attractive.[31] Maritain argues that since all perfections of the creature have their infinite source in God, there must be an analogue in the Godhead to that ennobling aspect of pain, what he calls "victorious acceptance", which we see in our fellow men. He finds this in an essential attribute for which there is no name, and which, unlike our suffering, involves no kind of imperfection; in fact, it is an integral part of the divine beatitude.[32]

The "essentialist" intuition of Maritain the philosopher needs to be extended and applied to the Trinitarian vitality of God. What makes possible the breadth and depth of Jesus' atoning suffering for us is the "recklessness" and "selflessness" with which, in the immanent Trinity, Father and Son eternally surrender themselves to each other in the Holy Spirit. "In the absolute self-surrender of the Father to the Son, of the Son to the Father, and of both to the Spirit, there are no 'safeguards' of any kind."[33] The Three Divine Persons are absolutely impassible and yet utterly defenceless; in their transparency to each other as subsistent relations, they are selves without self-protection. There is an "ever-open wound" at the heart of the Trinity identical to the eternal processions.[34] That is why when the Son becomes man, he takes the way of vulnerability and self-emptying, the lowly road that leads from Bethlehem to Golgotha. As man, with his human heart, the Son loves the Father and all mankind with an extravagance which mirrors the unbarriered "recklessness" of self-giving love within the Trinity. He suffers and dies as man at the hour when his unguarded love, divine and human, meets the hard palisade of calculating sinful selfishness.

14

The answer to the question whether there is suffering in God is this: in God is found the starting-point for what can become suffering when the recklessness (*Vorsichtslosigkeit*) with which the Father gives away himself (and *all* that is his) – which leads to the essentially divine recklessness of the total self-indebtedness and prodigal self-giving of the Son and that of the Spirit given to him – meets a freedom which does not respond to this recklessness.[35]

And the prodigality is unceasing. The glorified Lamb stands for ever "as slain" beside the Father (Apoc. 5:6). And until the end of the age, he pours himself out, gives us his whole substance, his holy sacrifice, in the Eucharist.

So, Balthasar concludes, God is neither mythically mutable/passible nor philosophically immutable/impassible.[36] In words that reveal his Ignatian heart and mind, he says that God is "ever greater" (*Deus semper maior*), infinitely above any conception or idea we form of him. He is not subject to the imperfections of creaturely suffering and change, but he is also more glorious than the words "immutable" or "impassible" by themselves imply. These negative terms express not a void or lack in God (as if God were lethargic or unfeeling), but rather the infinite richness and vitality of the intra-Trinitarian life. God is not mutable as creatures are, but neither is he immutable as creatures are. According to Adrienne, whose thought on this matter has exercised considerable influence on Balthasar, God's absolute immutability is both "true and absurd".

True, if the concept of "immutability" is measured by human standards. Completely untrue if one considers the true relation between God and the world: the fact that God infinitely transcends the

world and at the same time is immanent within it.
Now, in some incomprehensible way, change is
given a place in the heart of immutability . . . One
ought to say: with respect to any mutability within
creation there is in God from eternity a "supra-
mutability", which is "more than a match" for the
mutability of creation. In other words, it creates no
difficulty for God, it does not bring him into any
kind of dependence. When we use our concepts
"mutable/immutable", our standards are too small;
the reality is much fuller than we can imagine.[37]

In the Three-Personed God there is "an unimaginable
freedom which enables him to do more and to be
other than what the creature (on the basis of the
notions it has of God) would suppose of him".[38]

What, then, are we to say of this doctrine of the
divine attributes? Its strength is its ontology of relation and person, which balances the more substance-
based metaphysics of the Scholastics.[39] Balthasar sees
that impassibility and immutability are perfections of
a divine nature that is Triune, for, as St Thomas says,
in the Godhead, while the Three Persons are really
distinct from each other, their Persons are really
identical with their one divine nature; were this not
so, there would be four, not three, in God.[40] Whatever
else they mean, says Balthasar, the terms "immutability" and "impassibility" point to the boundless viva-
city of the Three in One.

It seems to me that, though he distances himself
from St Thomas on a number of issues, much of what
Balthasar says is illuminated by reference to the
Angelic Doctor. For example, St Thomas argues that
not only mutability but immutability too must be
denied of God if it implies imperfection.[41] In this
sense, he would agree with Adrienne that ascription
of immutability to God is both "true and absurd".

16

Similarly, the notion of "supra-mutability" corresponds to the Thomist affirmation of divine immutability in the "way of eminence", by which one moves beyond the "way of negation", denying of God this or that imperfection, and instead tries to point above and beyond to his boundless excellence, the all-surpassing grandeur that our limited minds cannot grasp.[42] Father Michael Woods, in a recent study, shows how, for St Thomas, divine immutability indicates not just God's invariable self-identity but his "dynamic and boundless perfection as *ipsum esse subsistens*".

> Far from implying, therefore, that God may be somehow static or inert, the attribute of immutability directly signifies that God, as pure *esse*, is pure dynamic actuality.[43]

What Balthasar adds is to make explicit what St Thomas presupposes, namely, that the all-surpassing eminence, "ever-greaterness", of God is Trinitarian, for He Who Is is Triune love. The Trinity's unceasing immanent activity of knowing and loving is neither imperfectly mutable nor imperfectly immutable (*via negationis*), but rather something infinitely more wonderful and alive than even the most alluring aspects of creaturely change and changelessness (*via eminentiae*).[44]

CHRIST AND ANALOGY

The mysteries of March reveal the Trinity. Indeed, all Christ's human words and deeds open up the richness of God's Triune being. Balthasar speaks, in this connection, of a "Christological analogy of being".[1] Although the distinction between the two natures is not abolished by their hypostatic union, there is a certain likeness between them within the greater unlikeness. Moreover, precisely because they are united in the Trinitarian hypostasis of the Son, we can conclude that all he does or suffers in his human nature has its analogue in the divine nature of the Blessed Trinity. In fact, everything that is Christian and of Christ – the theological virtues (faith and hope as well as love), prayer, the Eucharist, even Confession – has its archetype, according to Balthasar, in the life of the Trinity. Four concepts are essential for understanding this christological analogy of being and thus the Trinitarian dimension of the Incarnation and Easter: mission, obedience, kenosis, and exegesis.

Mission

Mission or "sending" (*Sendung*) is the principal leitmotiv in the second part of Balthasar's theological trilogy, the *Theodramatik*, which considers revelation as a divine drama. The idea of a divine person being sent to be and do something in the world is an essentially dramatic idea, elevating and fulfilling "role" in the theatrical and psychological sense.[2] For the whole New Testament, Jesus is the eternal Son sent into the world by the Father. St Paul teaches this (cf. Rom. 8:3f; Gal. 4:4), as do the Synoptics (cf. Mt. 10:40; Lk. 4:43), but it is St John who speaks most frequently of the mission of the Son. Balthasar's thinking on this subject is, therefore, strongly Johannine, but not exclusively so, for "John's mission Christology is just the logical unpacking of what is already implied in the Synoptics, which testify to Jesus' unique awareness of being sent".[3]

In addition to St John, Balthasar owes much, by his own admission, to St Thomas' systematic exposition of the divine missions.[4] On the Thomist view, the temporal missions of the Son and the Spirit presuppose and manifest their eternal processions. The Son is sent by the Father inasmuch as he is eternally generated by the Father. The Holy Spirit is sent by Father and Son inasmuch as he is eternally breathed forth by them. The Father alone is not sent, just as he alone does not proceed, for he is the source and origin of the whole Godhead. The divine missions are the processions with an extrinsic effect, their "prolongation" in human history.

> "Mission" not only signifies procession from a principle, but includes the procession's temporal term as well. So a mission takes place only in time. In other words, the mission includes the eternal procession with the addition of something else, namely, an effect in time, for the relation of a divine person to his principle can only be eternal.[5]

From this Thomist definition Balthasar concludes that in Christ person and mission are identical. Who is Jesus? He is the sent Son. If we are to understand his self-consciousness aright, that is to say, his human awareness of his divine self, we must see it, in the first place, as the consciousness of being the eternal Son sent into the world by the Father, the One who defines himself entirely in relation to the Father in the Holy Spirit.[6] To know his mission in this ontological, Trinitarian sense is to know who he is, whence he comes, whither he goes, what he is meant to do.

> If . . . Jesus' whole knowledge of belonging to God is based on his mission, then we do not have to worry about how his human consciousness is related to his divine consciousness. The Father's command to reveal his divine fatherhood through his whole being, through his living and dying in and for the world, fills and occupies his consciousness to the brim.[7]

The incarnate Son never lacks the human knowledge of his mission, and thus of his divine self in relation to the Father: "the Son, even in His human form, has to know that He is the Father's eternal Son, and that, therefore, His *missio* is indivisibly continuous with His *processio*".[8]

The concept of mission links not only Christology and Trinity but all the mysteries of Christ's life: together they constitute his mission. The first mystery of March is mission: the Son is sent in the human nature which he takes from the Virgin (*misit Deus Filium suum factum ex muliere* (Gal. 4:4)). And this first stage of the mission already looks to its goal: he is sent in a vulnerable human nature in order to reveal the Father and his love to a fallen and wounded world. Being sent into this "ungodly and anti-godly" world leads him, therefore, to the Cross.[9]

The identity in Christ of mission and procession shows us that Christianity is at once a theological aesthetic, dramatic, and logic – adoration of God's beauty, conflict in blood, truth embodied.[10] Our Lord and Saviour is the consubstantial Son who proceeds from the Father as his Logos of Truth and is sent into a world held captive by the father of lies. And so he is slaughtered as the sacrificial Lamb, bearing in his soul and body the impact of God's anger at sin. But he rises from the dead, triumphant over Satan, sin and death, and ascends to his Father's right hand, where, in his pierced and glorified flesh, he is worshipped by the whole Church in heaven and on earth.

The Lamb is adored with God and as God, and yet he stands "as he had been slain". This shows the continuity of *processio* and *missio*. The *missio* is worshipped as much as the *processio*. The Lamb, as "the Logos of God", goes off on his mission in "a robe dipped with blood", to "rule with a rod of iron and tread the winepress of the fury of the wrath of Almighty God" (Apoc. 19:13–16).[11]

Obedience

The centre of the theology of Hans Urs von Balthasar and Adrienne von Speyr is the obedience of the incarnate Son to the Father. It is the thread that runs through the whole life of Jesus: from the Incarnation in Mary to his death for us on the Cross, the Son obeys the Father.

At the beginning of all his work there is found obedience: the readiness to let himself be disposed of by the Father according to his total will. This is a letting go, an indifference that never chooses this as opposed to that. Already the way from the bosom of the eternal Father to the womb of the temporal Mother is a path of obedience, the most difficult and consequential of ways, but one which is trod on mission from the Father: "See, I come to do your will" (Heb. 10:7).[12]

Moreover, according to Balthasar, Christ's obedience discloses the Trinity's life of love and provides the model and source for the obedience of Mary and the Church.

Adrienne and Balthasar detect an *a priori* obedience within the Trinity. Not only as incarnate, but in becoming incarnate, the Son in a certain sense obeys the Father.

> The Son of God becomes man in obedience, and his whole human life is an expression of his primary obedience, which is embedded in a mystery between the Son and the Father.[13]

Now this is problematic, as Balthasar himself confesses.[14] Strictly speaking, there is no obedience within the Trinity: Father, Son, and Holy Spirit are one substance, one God, and so possess only one divine will. The eternal decision that mankind be saved through the Incarnation and Cross is as much the Son's decision, as God, as it is the Father's and the Spirit's. To suggest that the Son as God obeyed the Father could be taken to imply either his subordination to him or a plurality of wills in the Godhead and therefore a division of the divine substance. The inner life of the Blessed Trinity is coequal love, not domination and subservience.[15]

The picture of a primordial obedience within the Trinity is a further application of the "Christological analogy of being". Christ's human obedience is grounded in his divine person and thus in his eternal relation to the Father in the Holy Spirit.[16] The archetype for obedience within the Trinity is the filial way (*tropos*) in which the Son possesses the one divine will: the readiness, receptivity, responsiveness of the One who is the Father's consubstantial Word, Image, and Expression.[17] With the divine will that he has received from the Father, the Son from eternity is willing to assume human nature and to suffer for sinful mankind on the Cross. This is analogical obedience. Obedience in the full sense as implying service and submission, duty and command, comes into operation with the Incarnation, when the Son assumes a complete human nature, including a human will. With that will he expresses his divine eternal love for the Father in the form of human obedience unto death, even death on the Cross. This is Balthasar's great Johannine insight: Christ's obedience as "the revelation in human form of the eternal love of the divine Son for his eternal Father, who has eternally begotten him out of love".[18] As Jesus says in the Farewell Discourse, "I do as the Father has commanded me, so that the world may know that I love the Father" (John 14:31).

Christ's obedience is truly Trinitarian, engaging all Three Persons: it is directed to the Father, but it is lived out in the Holy Spirit.[19] Just as, in the inner life of the Godhead, the Holy Spirit is the mutual love of Father and Son, so, in his manhood, the Son obeys the Father under the impulse of the Spirit, whose grace fills his human heart. According to the evangelists, the Spirit "guides" the Son, even "drives" him (cf. Mk. 1:12), to do the Father's will. Taking an analogy from religious life, Adrienne, followed by Balthasar, says that, for the Son as man, the Spirit is the "Rule" of the Father, the One who proposes to his human mind and heart the wishes of the Father, a rule that in the Passion becomes inexorable.[20]

Balthasar observes that the incarnate Son's relation to the Holy Spirit is not the same in the "state of his self-emptying" (*status exinanitionis*), that is to say, from his conception to his Descent into Hell, as it is after the Resurrection. From virgin womb to empty tomb there is a certain "inversion" of the divine processions: within the Godhead the Spirit proceeds from the Father and the Son as from one principle (or from the Father "through" the Son, as the Cappadocian-Byzantine tradition prefers to say); whereas in the womb of the Virgin the Son becomes man through the Spirit and is guided by him on his mission.[21] The Holy Spirit is both "in" and "above" the Son as man: in him as his very own; above him as the Rule of the Father.[22] The Spirit's being in Jesus is, according to Balthasar, the economic form of the *Filioque*.[23]

In the fifth century the Nestorian heretics claimed that the Holy Spirit was a merely external force in the life of the man Jesus. Against this, St Cyril of Alexandria, whose Pneumatology closely resembles the *Filioque* doctrine, emphasized that the Spirit is the Son's very *own*, the Spirit of the Son as well as of the Father. That is why Jesus as man possesses the Spirit "without measure".[24] Balthasar adds to this Patristic insight the recognition that, in the Lord's "kenotic" state, his "eternal spontaneity and disposal of the Spirit is, as it were, restricted to and concentrated in obedience to the fatherly Spirit", i.e. docility to the Spirit's guidance as making plain to him the will of the Father.[25]

The supreme act of Christ's obedience is his Passion. He is obedient to the Father unto death, even death on the Cross (cf. Phil. 2:8). Now crucified obedience, too, takes place "under the influence of the Holy Spirit". As the Epistle to the Hebrews says, Christ offers himself "through the eternal Spirit" to the Father (cf. Heb. 9:14). Balthasar follows St Thomas and the majority of Catholic exegetes, both ancient and modern, in seeing a reference here to the role of the Holy Spirit in Christ's sacrifice.[26]

In the prayer said by the priest at Mass immediately

before receiving Holy Communion, we are told that Christ's death brought life to the world "by the will of the Father and the cooperation of the Holy Spirit". St John in his gospel, when he describes the death of Our Lord, says that he "gave up the Spirit" (19:30). In the first place this means simply that Jesus expired, surrendering his created *human spirit*, his rational and immortal soul, into the hands of the Father. As Our Lord says in St Luke's gospel, "Father, into thy hands I commend my spirit" (Luke 23:46). Now it may be that here, as so often in the fourth gospel, there are several layers of meaning. Perhaps John wants us to see the *uncreated Holy Spirit*, the Third Person of the Trinity, as being in some sense "given" at the moment of Christ's sacrificial death – not bestowed on men (that, for John, takes place after the Resurrection, 20:22), but *returned to the Father*. This is Balthasar's and Adrienne's great intuition into the Johannine Passion narrative. Christ's obedience unto death is, as we have seen, the human form of his eternal love of the Father in the Spirit. What St John may, therefore, be saying is this: Our Lord's dying breath is one of love for the Father, sighed in perfect docility to the Holy Spirit. As Hugh of St Cher suggested in the thirteenth century, "not by fire, not by any sacrificial means of the old dispensation, but by the Holy Spirit directing and suggesting everything to him, he offered himself as an immaculate Victim through the Holy Spirit to God the Father".[27]

This exegesis helps us understand, according to Balthasar, St John's mysterious words about the Spirit not being given before Jesus was glorified (cf. 7:39). In the state of self-emptying, from Lady Day to Holy Saturday, the Holy Spirit is not, so to speak, "available" for others. His role is to guide and drive the Son on his mission of obedience. Only when the Son, by the motion of the Spirit, has breathed out his life and love for the Father and all mankind, only when the Father has accepted his Sacrifice and poured out the Spirit on his humanity in the Resurrection, only then can the risen Lord breathe the Spirit on the apostles (cf. John 20:22); only then can the Dove descend from the Father and the Son upon the whole Church at Pentecost (cf. Acts 2:2f.).[28] At the Incarnation the Spirit brought the Son into the world; at Easter the incarnate Son, through his bodily breath, brings the Spirit into the world.[29]

> [The Spirit] is only available when the [Son's] earthly mission has been accomplished. The Spirit is humanly breathed back to the Father at the moment of death (Mt. 27:50; Mk. 15:37; Lk. 23:46; Jn. 19:30), so that, at Easter, he can be breathed *into* the Church (Jn. 2:22) and at Pentecost can descend from the Father and the Son together upon the Church.[30]

Our Lord's bloody sacrifice on Calvary is Trinitarian in this sense: it is the incarnate Son's offering of himself, his soul and body, to the Father in the Holy Spirit. Holy Mass, in which that sacrifice is made really present and offered in a sacramental and unbloody way, likewise has a Trinitarian structure: it is an oblation of the immaculate Victim by his Church to God the Father in the Holy Spirit.[31]

Christ's obedience is both the "exegesis" of the Trinity's life of love and the "epitome" of the creature's proper attitude to God, and especially that of the Church, his Body and Bride. As Christ in the Spirit obeys the Father, so the Church in the Spirit is to obey Christ. Obedience is once again the incarnation of love. The Head asks his members to show their love for him by doing what he commands: "If a man loves me, he will keep my word, and my Father will love him, and we will come to him and make our home

26

with him" (John 14:23). Such obedience on the part of the individual Christian is not a solitary act; on the contrary, it is profoundly ecclesial.

> [Obedience] . . . connects us in faith to the will of Christ in his obedience to the Father, and by the same token connects us to the faithful obedience to Christ of the Church, his Bride, who, in her spirit of faithful obedience, is our mother and teacher.[32]

The man who wants to have the mind of Christ strives, in the Spirit, to think with the Church, to have her disposition as devoted Bride. Such an undertaking would be a romantic dream were the Church merely a collective organization. But, in fact, in Mary, the Church, as Bride and Virgin Mother, is a person. To obey Christ as we should, with the disposition of the Church, means having the attitude of Mary. For she is the supreme example of the loving obedience to Jesus and his Father of which St John's gospel speaks. By her Yes to God, she is not only the model for the Church's obedience, in a very real sense she *is* the readily obedient Church, Christ's Bride and our Mother. So the hallmark of Christian spirituality must be "obedience in the Marian Church to the Lord and in the Lord to the Father in the Holy Spirit".[33]

Balthasar marries the doctrine of his patron St John the Evangelist to the insights of the man he always called "our holy father" (*sanctus pater noster*), St Ignatius Loyola.[34] St John's is the great gospel of obedience, and Ignatius, the founder of the Society of Jesus, of which Balthasar was a member for over twenty years, is the great down-to-earth doctor of ecclesial obedience: obeying Christ means obeying the Pope and our superiors in God, wholeheartedly assenting to the Church's teaching, praising and thanking God for all that he gives us in the real, visible Roman Catholic Church.

Kenosis

According to St Paul, the Son of God, in becoming man, did not "cling to his equality with God, but emptied Himself (*heauton ekenôse*), taking the form of a servant" (Phil. 2:6f.). He who is coequal with the Father in his divine "form" does not "think of that form as a precious, inalienable, private possession to be clung to",[35] but assumes our lowly human form, in which he is less than the Father, in which he serves and obeys the Father "unto death, even death on the cross" (v. 8). He is "so divinely free that he can tie himself down to slavish obedience".[36] Balthasar's great insight, which, by his own admission, owes much to the Russian Orthodox theologian, Sergei Bulgakov, is that the "kenosis" of the Incarnation is made possible by and lays open a preceding and underlying kenosis within the Trinity.

> The ultimate presupposition of the kenosis is the "selflessness" of the [divine] persons in the intra-Trinitarian life of love.[37]

When applied to the immanent Trinity, the word "kenosis", traditionally predicated of the Incarnation, is being used analogically, not univocally.[38] Incarnational kenosis is the assumption of a passible and mortal human nature by the Son; Trinitarian kenosis concerns the immanent giving and receiving of the impassible and immortal divine nature of the Three Divine Persons. In assuming our humanity, God the Son does not "cling to his divinity", but then none of the Divine Persons cling to the divinity in the inner life of the Trinity. The Father does not hug the Godhead to himself (as the Scrooge-like God of the Arians does) but, by eternal generation, lavishes it upon the consubstantial Son, who receives it with a response of grateful, Eucharistic love.[39] And Father and Son do not clasp the divine essence in an *égoïsme à deux* but communicate it, without remainder, to the Holy Spirit, who proceeds from them as their mutual breath of love. In all this giving and receiving, there is no "before" or "after", no "greater" or "less". The Father does not exist "before" he gives himself. He is this self-giving movement.

> He does not share [the divinity] with the Son, but communicates all that is his to the Son: "All thine is mine" (Jn. 17:10). Of course, we must not think in an Arian way of the Father existing "before" this self-giving. He is this self-giving movement, without holding anything back in a calculating way.[40]

The personal being (*esse personale*) of the Father is a being towards the Son, an *esse ad*. The Three Divine Persons, the Three Divine Selves, are selfless: they are pure relations. None of them exists privately or in isolation. Whoever each of them is, he is in relation to the others: the Father is the Father of the Son; the Son is the Son of the Father; the Spirit is the Common Spirit of Father and Son, the "subsistent We" of the paternal I and filial Thou.[41] In the being of God there is a mysterious identity of wealth and poverty.

> Poverty does not exist before wealth, as if God could only be himself by going through the Trinitarian process (as Idealism thinks). Nor does wealth exist before poverty, as if the Father (the One) existed eternally for himself before generating the Son (as Arianism, inspired by Platonism, thought).[42]

This, then, is the Trinitarian kenosis: God in himself is a consubstantial communion of selfless, self-emptied persons. In a word, God is love, Triune love. He does not lose anything in the dance of dispossession: only

29

thus is he God.[43] In the Trinity having and giving away are one.

> The Father, who begets the Son, does not "lose" himself in that act to Another in order only thus to "attain" himself; it is precisely as the One who gives himself that he *always* is himself. And the Son, too, is always himself by letting himself be begotten and letting the Father have him at his disposal. The Spirit is always himself by seeing his "I" as the "We" of Father and Son, making this expropriation his *propriissimum*. (It is only when we understand this that we escape from the machinery of Hegel's dialectic).[44]

And this is the God revealed in and through Christ. The Father does not cling to his Son but sacrifices him for us all. The Son does not cling to his equality with the Father but, in his human nature, gives himself, lets himself be given – for us on the Cross, to us in the Eucharist. And Father and Son do not cling to their Holy Spirit but pour him into our hearts to draw us into communion with themselves and with each other in the one Mystical Body.[45]

> [God's] sovereignty is shown, not in clinging to what is his own, but in giving it away. It is a sovereignty that extends far beyond the opposition, in worldly terms, between power and powerlessness. God's self-emptying [in the Incarnation] is ontically possible because of God's eternal emptiedness, his Three-Personed self-giving.[46]

The kenosis of the Incarnation and the Cross is preceded by, in Balthasar's opinion, a kenosis in creation itself. This is the first outward showing of the inward self-emtying of the Divine Persons.

A fundamental kenosis is involved in creation in the

sense that God from eternity has taken responsibility for its success (for human freedom, too) and, in his foreseeing of sin, has "taken account" of the Cross (as the foundation of creation): "Christ's Cross is inscribed into the creation of the world from its foundation" (Bulgakov). Finally, in the real world of sinners, "his redeeming Passion begins at the same time as his Incarnation". Since the will that wills the redemptive kenosis is the inseparably Triune will, God the Father and the Holy Spirit are engaged in the most serious way in the kenosis, according to Bulgakov: the Father as sender and forsaker, the Spirit as the One who unites in and through separation and absence.[47]

According to the constant teaching of the Church, as expressed, for example, in the Dogmatic Constitution *Dei Filius* of the First Vatican Council, God created the world by a will free of all necessity or pressure.[48] Not even his own goodness obliged him to create.[49] Creation is, therefore, an act of breathtakingly disinterested love. It is, we might add, an act of "unclinging", kenotic love. There is nothing possessive or acquisitive about it; as St Thomas says, "[God] alone is supremely liberal, since he does not act for his own benefit, but solely because of his goodness".[50] Now, according to Balthasar, the selfless generosity of the creative act is a fitting (not necessary) disclosure of the selfless life of love of the Trinity.

> The life of the Trinity is an eternally self-fulfilled circle, which does not need the world . . . The act of creation has its source in the freedom of the Trinity; it is a "selfless" sharing of [the Trinity's] life of blessed selflessness with needy creatures.[51]

Bonum est diffusivum sui: goodness bubbles over, pours, empties itself out. That is first of all necessarily true of the uncreated inner life of the Trinity before being fittingly shown forth in the freely loving gift that is creation.[52]

Creation manifests the Trinitarian kenosis in another way. God has not just freely made a world; he has freely made a world of finite freedom, that is to say, rational creatures capable of genuine interaction with him as players on the stage of history,[53] persons who are freely and distinctly themselves, thereby sharing, in a creaturely way, in the Son's role within the Godhead as Expression of the Father, as Thou to the paternal I.[54] Of course, this freedom can be, and in Adam is, misused, so that creaturely difference becomes sinful distance from God. But how can an infinitely good God permit such dangerously fallible freedom? Balthasar's answer is that since the difference, "the absolute, infinite distance", between the Father and Son is bridged by and in the Holy Spirit, the Father can not only make creatures to be different but permit them, though of course not will them, to be distant. The Trinity is absolute unity in absolute diversity, and so however far a creature may remove himself from God, he is never beyond the loving arms of the Father. For the Son, who loves the Father in the Holy Spirit, is from eternity ready to assume human nature and so go off into Godforsakenness to bring mankind back to the Trinity.

> The divine act [of generation] which produces the Son . . . establishes an absolute, infinite distance, within which all other possible distances, as they may emerge within the finite world, including sin, are enclosed and encircled.[55]

The analogical kenosis of the divine relations is what makes possible all the other kenoses – creation, covenant, and redemptive Incarnation.

The first "self-limitation" of the Triune God because of the freedom given to the creature; the second, deeper "self-limitation" of the same Triune God through his Covenant, which on God's side is from the beginning indissoluble, whatever Israel might do; and the third kenosis is not only Christological but involves the whole Trinity through the Incarnation of the Son alone, who shows clearly to the world his eternal Eucharistic attitude in the *pro nobis* of the Cross and Resurrection.[56]

In using the term "kenosis" analogically to describe the selfless Trinitarian love that God is, we must avoid any suggestion that the other kenoses take place by some kind of necessity, as if the kenotic Trinity were bound to create and redeem in a kenotic way. That is the error of Gnosticism and Idealism. No, the kenoses of creation, Incarnation, and Cross are works of divine freedom. The kenosis is voluntary, as the Fathers always insist.

Nothing but his infinitely free love can lead God to create the world or to redeem it in this most wonderful way. And though the "economic" manifestation of the intra-Trinitarian mystery reveals to us something of the immanent law of the Trinity, it is nonetheless impossible to deduce from that inner law any kind of necessity about this manifestation. Only when the mystery of divine love has been disclosed in Jesus Christ do we have the right to conclude that God could do what in fact he really did do, that his abasement and dispossession do not contradict his own essence, but – in an unsuspected way – were in complete harmony with it.[57]

The incarnational kenosis is a work not only of divine freedom but of divine omnipotence. God's almightiness "blazes forth", says Balthasar, "in the powerlessness of the incarnate and crucified Son".[58] The greatest work of almighty God is his assumption of our weakness in the womb of the Virgin and his death in that weakness on the Cross. In the glorious words of St Gregory of Nyssa:

> All-powerful nature's capacity to descend to the lowliness of the human condition is a far greater proof of power than the miracles of an imposing and supernatural kind . . . The humiliation of God shows the superabundance of his power, which is not in any way hindered in the midst of these conditions contrary to his nature . . . The grandeur is manifested in lowliness without being degraded by it.[59]

Exegesis

"No one has ever seen God", says St John, "the only Son, who is in the bosom of the Father, he has made him known" (John 1:18). The Greek word here translated as "to make known" means "to expound, to explain, to reveal". It is the verb from which the noun "exegesis" is derived. So what St John is saying here, in Balthasar's view, is that the Only-Begotten has become man to reveal his Father, to be his *Exegete*.[60]

The incarnate Word reveals the Father, Balthasar reminds us, in his whole human existence – in his childhood as well as in his adulthood, by his works as well as his words, by his silence as well as his speech, by his sufferings as well as his actions. The paradoxical eloquence of the silent Word particularly haunts Balthasar's imagination. Like the Fathers before him, he is stunned by the Christmas mystery of a *Verbum infans*, the divine Word who has become *in-fans*, a baby who cannot speak. The Word is made flesh at the moment of his conception in the Virgin's womb, and so his revealing work begins in the hiddenness and silence of his Mother's body.

> Before birth, nine months of development pass by in the deepest silence. Since the event of the Word becoming flesh takes place precisely at conception, the Word becomes man by making himself silence.[61]

This still intimacy of the unborn Logos with his Mother is the model for Christian contemplation.[62]

Silence also has a place in the teaching of the grown-up Jesus. First, as the gospels bear witness, his public ministry is regularly punctuated by prayer in the desert. In other words, his human words proceed from his silent contemplation of the Father. This is a beautiful silence. But there is something else in his ministry, a harsher, more chilling muteness. His hearers do not hear him and freeze into guilty silence. Balthasar calls the disputes in St John's gospel a "dialogue of the deaf".[63] "Ears have they, but hear not" (Jer. 5:21; cf. Matt. 13:13). In his Passion, on trial before Caiaphas, Herod and Pilate, Jesus speaks "only through his silence".[64] He makes no answer, and his judges "wonder" (cf. Mark 15:5). Finally, on the Cross the incarnate Word dies with a wordless "loud voice" (*voce magna*, Matt. 27:50). This inarticulate cry Balthasar regards as the supreme utterance of the Word, the disclosure of the ultimate truth of the Father. The "centre of the Word", speaking volumes, is an apparent "non-word".[65]

Balthasar's theology of the eloquent silence of the Word in his infancy and Passion has affinities with the mysterious assertion of St Ignatius of Antioch in his epistle to the Ephesians that the virginal conception, birth, and death of the Lord are 'three loud-crying mysteries accomplished in silence".[66] The human speechlessness is a fitting expression of the divine silence in which, according to Ignatius, the Word "comes forth", that is to say, is eternally uttered, generated, by the Father.[67] "Silence" here is a metaphor for the ever-greater transcendence of the generation of the Word, its unlikeness to vocal utterance or physical birth. This ever-greatness of the procession *ad intra* is fittingly manifested in the actual human silence of the incarnate Word on Calvary, in the poverty and obscurity in which he dies. Once again, we see how the eternal procession is manifested in the temporal mission. The centurion hears the message contained in Jesus' last non-word and says, in archetypal faith: "Truly this man was the Son of God" (cf. Mark 15:39). But the silence of the Word does not even end there, for, having given himself up with a great cry into the "mute hands" of the Father, he descends into the abyssal silence of death, of Sheol, and there he is "the wordless yet resounding Word".[68] "God cannot proclaim himself more loudly than when he reaches down to be with us in our very lostness".[69] Even the grave's terrible silence has been assumed, for our salvation, by the Word.

From Lady Day to the Last Day and for ever, the incarnate Word is the "Exegete" of the Father; even silent, he is, in a phrase of Shakespeare's, "the perfectest herald" of God. When Jesus cries out and surrenders his Spirit to the Father, "the Father speaks his loudest and most definitive word: 'God so loved the world that he gave his only Son'".[70] As a gloss on that Johannine text, Balthasar frequently cites these fine words of the medieval monastic writer, William of St Thierry:

And everything he did and everything he said on earth, even the insults, the spitting, the buffeting, the Cross and the grave, all that was nothing but yourself speaking in the Son, appealing to us by your love, and stirring up our love for you.[71]

If the incarnate Son is the Exegete of the Father, the Holy Spirit is the Exegete of the Son, or, more accurately, his "Eisegete", the One who gives us our entry to the filial exegesis of the paternal mystery. Jesus, the incarnate Son, is the way to the Father, but the Spirit is the way to the Son, the One who guides us into all the truth that is Jesus (cf. John 16:13).[72]

The Spirit is not a second exegesis of God, but only the completion of the first and only one, for "he will not speak on his own authority, but . . . will take what is mine and declare it to you".[73]

The Holy Spirit, the Spirit of the Son as well as of the Father, is never a Spirit of disincarnation.

It must never be forgotten that the expounding Spirit works as the One who "takes from what is mine", and "what is mine" is permanently incarnate. So His testimony is only ever given with water and blood. And though the Spirit himself is revealed as a divine water for us to drink, as a living spring welling up to eternal life (John 7.38), Christ's living blood must also be drunk with it (John 6:65f).[74]

The Spirit "blows where he wills" (cf. John 3:8), but "where he wills" is always back to Jesus. This explains the so-called "anonymity" of the Spirit. He has no face in Christian iconography, only the visible yet enigmatic form of the dove, the flame, the wind. The Spirit-Finger of God always points to Jesus.

The Holy Spirit never points to himself, never puts himself in the light. He is always the Spirit of the

Son and of the Father. On their love his light falls, without disclosing its source as such.[75]

And his exposition of Jesus is never disembodied or abstract. It is in the Church, Christ's Mystical Body, with her tradition, scriptures, magisterium, and seven sacraments that the Spirit expounds the Son. As St Irenaeus says, "Where the Church is, there too is the Spirit of God, and where the Spirit of God, there is the Church and all grace; and the Spirit is truth".[76] The Paraclete takes what belongs to the Son and declares it to us (cf. John 16:14). He never takes us away from, but only ever more deeply into, the incarnate reality of Jesus. He is in agreement, as St John makes clear, with the water and the blood (cf. 1 John 5:8). That is why the epiclesis of the Spirit in the Eucharistic Prayer is paradigmatic for an understanding of his work. There the Church prays the Father to send his Spirit to change bread and wine into the Body and Blood of his Son. The Spirit is inseparable from the crucified and risen flesh of the Son. His streams flow down to us through the wounded Heart of Jesus, and through that same channel their ebb bears us back to the Father. Transubstantiation is, therefore, the classic instance of the Spirit's operation.

4
INCARNATE AND CRUCIFIED FOR US

According to the New Testament and the Nicene Creed, the Son of God became man, died, and rose again "for us" (*hyper hêmôn*, *pro nobis*). For Balthasar, these two little words are the "first and most fundamental words of the Christian faith",[1] but he feels that certain interpretations of them fall seriously short of their full meaning. *Pro nobis* means, for example, much more than "for the benefit of", more than "in solidarity with" or "instead of us because we were unable". These definitions are all true and necessary for an understanding of Redemption, but they are insufficient. What, then, is the deeper level of meaning? It is this: Balthasar claims that, when the Church confesses that the incarnate Son suffered and died "for us", she means that he *changed places with us*. Our costly redemption was a work of *substitution*.

The New Testament Witness

In unfolding Christ's saving work, Balthasar confronts some of the New Testament's hardest texts, in particular, St Paul's astounding declaration that "for us [God the Father] made [Christ] to be sin who knew no sin, so that in him we might become the righteousness of God" (2 Cor. 5:21). The sinless Son has put himself in the position of sinners, so that they can be repositioned in the bosom of the Father as sons in the Son. The Innocent, the Holy of Holies, in some mysterious way places his shoulders beneath the hideous weight of our guilt, so that we may stand upright in the glorious freedom of the children of God. Here is the most dramatic gesture in that "wonderful commerce" (*admirabile commercium*) which began in the womb of the Virgin, when the Son of God took the poverty of our humanity and gave us in exchange the riches of his divinity (cf. 2 Cor. 8:9).[2] On Calvary, as St Ephrem says, "the Kind One . . . let us take the truth, while he from us took sin".[3]

> He experiences instead of us what distance from God is, so that we may become beloved and loving children of God instead of being his "enemies" (Rom. 5:10).[4]

In expounding the substitutive meaning of the *pro nobis*, Balthasar does not want to reduce the mystery of the Cross to a formula. In this he resembles St Thomas, whom he applauds for insisting that no single concept can express the infinitely rich meaning of Christ's saving Passion.[5] In the New Testament, Balthasar isolates five main aspects of the Atonement. The first two concern the act of redemption itself: (1) the *giving up* of the Son by the Father (together with his willingness to be given up as Lamb and his own active self-offering as Priest); (2) the *change of places* between the sinless Son and sinful mankind. The third and fourth describe the purpose of the redemptive act: (3) man's *liberation* from sin and death and the powers of evil; and (4) his *insertion into the divine life of the Trinity*. The fifth is the source from which all this proceeds: (5) the *love* that the Blessed Trinity is.[6] The aim of any soteriology deserving of the name "Catholic" should be to help the believer to see the wonder of Redemption in all these five dimensions.

This five-dimensional reading of the New Testament distinguishes Balthasar's understanding of
substitution from that of the Reformers, which it
might appear to resemble. Luther and Calvin recognize that the Son is given up by the Father and
changes places with us sinners (New Testament
themes (1) and (2)), but they fail to show how everything proceeds from, indeed manifests, the Triune
God of love (5). For, in their theory, the innocent
Jesus is *punished* in our place by God the Father.
Balthasar rejects any suggestion of *penal* substitution.

> There is no sense in which we can say that God the
> Father "punishes" the suffering Son in our place.
> There can be no question of punishment, for the
> work accomplished here between Father and Son
> with the cooperation of the Holy Spirit is pure love,
> love most undefiled, and therefore a supremely
> voluntary work, on the part of the Son as much as
> on the part of the Father and the Spirit. The love of
> God is so rich that it can assume even this form of
> darkness out of love for our dark world.[7]

The Christology of the Church

Balthasar's theology of the *pro nobis* presupposes and
builds upon the orthodox Christology and Trinitarian
doctrine of the Church. First, it presupposes that the
subject of the Passion is a divine person. It is as man,
in his human nature, that he suffers and dies for us,
but he who suffers and dies is God, God the Son,
"One of the Trinity". And because he is God, his
human sufferings have an inclusiveness, a breadth
and depth, which no ordinary man's could have. It is
his very uniqueness as the God-Man, as the man who
is God, that is the ground of his all-embracing

relationships with men as Head and Second Adam. It is as man, but because he is God, that he is able to substitute himself, to take upon himself the unbearable burden of the whole world's guilt.

> This absolutely unique Man . . . is unique precisely because he is God. And for this and for no other reason, he can give a share in his once-for-all Cross to his fellow human beings, with whom he is in deeper solidarity than any man could ever be with another. He can give them, in other words, a share in his death, where every man otherwise is absolutely alone.[8]

Only One of the Trinity can as man die "for all" (cf. 2 Cor. 4:14f).[9] The uniqueness of his Trinitarian person is the ground of Christ's all-embracing solidarity with and substitution for men. He is the universal Word, through, with and for whom all things were made, and is able to communicate something of his universality to the human nature united to his divine person without robbing it of its particularity. The Son's vicarious act of reconciliation is, therefore, both exclusive and inclusive.[10] Insofar as the sinless God-Man does what we cannot do, it is exclusive; but in so far as he stands in for us as our Head, it is inclusive. In other words, mankind, for whose sins he makes satisfaction by his Passion, has been put into a new situation *in its very being*, even before it acknowledges the fact by faith.[11]

The Sinless Son

St Paul says that it is the One that "knows no sin" who becomes sin. Were Jesus not the absolutely sinless Son, he could not take upon himself the sin of the world, for sin is the very opposite of solidarity and substitution.[12] The more a man is attached to sin the less capable he is of putting himself, whether in thought or reality, in the place of his brethren. The sinner is too enclosed within the prison of selfishness to be capable of self-outpouring love. In any case, no mere man, even the greatest saint, can bear and bear away the vast load of the world's guilt.

> The One who suffers the night is the absolutely Innocent One: no other person would be capable of enduring it in this efficacious and vicarious way. What ordinary man, or extraordinary man for that matter, could find room within himself for the guilt of the world? Only One person has that much room within himself: the One who lives in divine distance in relation to the Father, i.e. the Son, who, even as man, is God.[13]

There can be no question, then, of the Crucified identifying himself with the actual No of sin itself. Jesus is always pure loving Yes to the Father, and so his vicarious experience of sin's darkness cannot be like that of God-hating sinners. But the unlikeness does not attenuate his pain. On the contrary, his absolute sinlessness enables him to suffer as man more deeply, more intensely, than any sinful human person ever could. The sinner can always protect himself with a shield of self-pity, whereas the selfless Trinitarian person of the Son, in all his human pain, is turned outwards to the Father and to his brethren. Through its hypostatic union with his divine person, his human heart is open and vulnerable, incapable of uncompassion.

> The darkness of the state of sin is experienced by Jesus in a way that cannot be identical with what (God-hating) sinners inevitably experience . . . In fact, Jesus' experience is deeper and darker than

43

theirs, because it takes place within the depths of the relationship of the divine hypostases, a depth which no creature can have any sense of.[14]

It is sin's very unfamiliarity that causes the sin-bearing Lamb such pain. Unlike the guilty, the Innocent sees the *peccatum mundi* for what it is – God-offending and man-destroying.

> The crucified Jesus suffers, in our place, our interior estrangement from God and our experience of God's darkness; indeed, it is so painful because it is so undeserved. For him, there is nothing familiar about it; it is all that is absolutely alien and horrible. Yes, he suffers something deeper than any ordinary man can, even one condemned and cast out from God, because only the Son, the Incarnate One, knows in truth who the Father is and what it means to go without him, to have lost him apparently for ever. It makes no sense to call this suffering Hell, for in Jesus there is no kind of hatred of God, only a pain which is deeper and also more timeless than what an ordinary man in life or after death might endure.[15]

Balthasar enlarges an argument offered by St Thomas for Our Lord's Passion being greater than all or any other human pain. The primary cause of his interior suffering was, says St Thomas, "all the sins of the human race, for which he was making satisfaction by his Passion. And so it is as if he is ascribing them to himself (*unde ea quasi sibi adscribit*) when he refers (in Psalm 21:2) to 'the words of my sins'".[16] Balthasar comments:

> Christ no longer wants to distinguish between himself and his guilty brethren. Notice that *adscribit* is an active verb. We must suppose . . . in the passive Passion, willed and commanded by God, a

sovereign spontaneity of Jesus, who, at the head of all those who will follow him, takes his Cross upon himself (Lk. 8:23; 14:27), that Cross whose weight is out of all proportion to his human powers on their own. It will crush him, and more spiritually than physically.[17]

Our Lord identifies himself with sinful mankind as suffering sin not as committing it. As George Herbert says of the Agony in the Garden, "Sinne is that presse and vice, which forceth pain/ To hunt his cruell food through ev'ry vein". Obedient to the Father, loving us into the depths, Christ, with his human will, lets the monstrous, crushing weight of the world's sin fall upon him. All the pains merited by men's wickedness he lovingly takes upon himself, not as punishment but as satisfaction and expiation. The holy Lamb wants to bear and thus bear away this hideous insult to his Father's goodness, this source of all human woe.

> [Christ gathers] up into himself . . . the world's sin, which offends the goodness of the Father, in order to burn it utterly in the fire of his suffering. The Father is henceforth to perceive this sin as being only fuel for the Son's love: "Behold the Lamb of God [the scapegoat], who takes away the sin of the world [into the desert, into a place which is out of sight and unreachable]".[18]

In soul and in body, he experiences the sin of the world, feels, as no thick-skinned sinner could ever feel, the collective violence of every human No to God. And so his bodily sufferings – the scourge, the thorns, the nails, the thirst – become a kind of "perverse sacrament that effects interiorly what it signifies in the external image: the sufferings which are being driven into the body of Jesus are in truth the sins of the world, knocked forcibly into his total divine and human person".[19] When the Son is nailed to the Cross, says Adrienne, "the whole immense sum of the world's sin penetrates his body through the wounds".[20] Never was grief like this.

Godforsaken For Us

The climax of Our Lord's substitutive Passion is his abandonment by the Father, loudly voiced in the words *Eli, Eli lama sabachthani*, "My God, my God, why hast thou forsaken me?" (Matt. 27:46). He wants to love sinful mankind "to the end" (cf. John 13:1), into the depths, to the utmost and outermost, even into Godforsakenness.

The cry of dereliction is not one of despair or protest but "of obedience".[21] Jesus is Godforsaken for the sake of the Father. God the Father so loves mankind that he wants his Son as man to let go of his intimacy with him, to "[bear] all the estrangement that the world's sin involves (John 1:29) and through his obedience [overcome] it (John 16:33)". And to this terrible task the Son says Yes. The Father has accompanied him throughout his mission: at every moment of his human existence, from his conception in the Virgin's womb, he has lived in the near presence and direct vision of the Father. But now, on Good Friday, in obedience to the Father's loving plan, out of love for mankind in its misery, he "renounces all perceptible contact with the Father in order to experience in himself the sinner's distance from God – and no one can be more abandoned by the Father than the Son, because no one knows him and lives in so much dependence on him as the Son".[22] For the love of the Father, the Son renounces the experience of his love and is left with nothing but hard, blind obedience.

46

Even when Fatherforsaken, he is Father-centred. Plunged into a spiritual darkness deeper than any mystic's night, he still surrenders himself: "Father, into thy hands I commend my spirit" (Luke 23:46). This is the self-offering, the sacrifice, that makes our peace with God.

Here we encounter the paradox of the "hour", the goal of Jesus' life on earth. It is the hour of the Father, when the Son glorifies and shows his love for him, but it is also the hour of darkness, calling for "an identification with that far-from-God darkness which the sinner reaches by his No".[23] The pit into which the sinner falls by his No, the Son reaches by his Yes. The "Passover" of the Son, his "Exodus" from this world to the Father (cf. John 13:1), is the translation in his humanity of his eternal response of grateful love to his begetting by the Father. Paradoxically, this movement towards the Father takes him, in the fallen world he has come to redeem, into what is furthest from the Father. So while the hour is something the incarnate Son can affirm and accept freely in advance, it also appears to him as a totally excessive demand, to be faced in weakness and dread. "Now is my soul troubled. And what shall I say? 'Father, save me from this hour?' No, for this purpose I have come to this hour. Father, glorify thy name" (John 12:27f.).[24]

The Son's obedient embracing of Godforsakenness is a work of substitution. He endures desolation for us, as our Head and in our place. He enters into solidarity with all who feel abandoned and forgotten by God. In what the Greek Fathers boldly called his "foolish" love of mankind, God wants to experience the absence of God.[25] He suffers an abandonment infinitely more wounding than that of sinners, one that somehow embraces theirs, bringing light into the midnight of their anguish, placing pierced hands of love beneath their fall. There are no uncharted territories. Even in the most hellish deserts of this life, no man need despair. Godforsakenness, too, can be a holy place, for it has been hallowed and made hopeful by the person and presence of God incarnate himself. His substitutive Passion effects a "transplantation", an ontological change of position for mankind.

> The transplantation in question is real. It establishes a new ontology of man, who henceforth is "incorporated in the Kingdom of the beloved Son".[26]

Confession For Us

Perhaps the most original insight of Adrienne and Balthasar into the mystery of what Christ does "for us" on the Cross concerns Confession. As the Head and representative of all humanity, the Son confesses all our sins to the Father on the Cross and receives forgiveness for us, when the Father raises him from the tomb on Easter Day. By breathing the Holy Spirit on them, the risen Son gives the power of absolution to his apostles, for they are to share in and continue his own mission from the Father.[27]

The Sacrament of Penance has its deepest foundations in the immanent Trinity: in the Son's utter transparency to the Father in the Holy Spirit.[28] This takes human form, through the Incarnation, in the complete openness of his created mind and heart to the Father in the Spirit. He wants to show everything, offer everything, to the Father.[29] This is of immense consolation to the penitent. If, as St Paul says, we do not know how to pray as we ought (cf. Rom. 8:26), so we only ever confess in broken, halting words. We need the grace of Christ to confess just as we need that grace to pray. The Spirit who catches us up into the eternal dialogue of Father and Son when we pray takes us, when we confess to a priest, into the perfect, unfaltering confession of the sinless Son. The heart of the penitent's disposition is a Yes of faith clothed in a humble sense of need.

People only really confess in unconnected words; but in Hell he learnt how to cope with unconnectedness. It is as if he knew the whole text (say, of a poem), of which penitents only ever say the first word of the verse. He knows the poem; the meaning lies in him, the one who listens. The other person, the one who recites it, is only a bungler.[30]

Substitution and the Trinity

The Son's substitution for mankind on the Cross manifests Trinitarian love. First, it shows the Trinity's love towards us: the Father loves us so much that he does not spare his only Son but gives him up even to Godforsakenness for us all (cf. John 3:16; Rom. 8:32). The incarnate Son, with his human heart, wants to love us "to the end" (cf. John 13:1). But that is not all. Behind this manward love of Father and Son is the inward mutual love of Father and Son in the Holy Spirit. That too, that above all, is displayed on the Cross. The Son's bearing of our sins is an act of human obedience and expresses his eternal, divine love of the Father. He wants to do all he can to renew the Father's fallen creation. And the Father, in sending the Son into the world he made through him, expresses his loving wish that all things should be crowned and summed up in him.

This love *must* be twofold: the love of God the Father permitting God the Son to go, in absolute obedience, poverty, and self-abandonment, to where he can be no more than pure receptivity to

49

the divine "wrath"; and the love of God the Son
who, out of love, identifies himself with us sinners
(Heb. 2:13), and thereby, through his free obedience, accomplishes the will of the Father (Heb.
10:7). Only this double love provides the key to
understand the mystery.[31]

The drama of Calvary uncurtains the drama of love
within the Triune Godhead. We have already said
something of how incarnational self-emptying presupposes intra-Trinitarian selflessness. Similarly, the
vicarious or substitutive aspect of the incarnate Son's
death on the Cross opens up an analogical "substitution and exchange" of the Three in One. Catholic
tradition has given this the name *perichorêsis* or *circu-
mincessio*, the Greek and Latin words, respectively, for
the mutual indwelling and interpenetration of the
Divine Persons in the one substance. On the Cross,
we have said, the Innocent puts himself in the Godforsaken position of the guilty, so that they may be
repositioned in him as his Father's adopted sons and
daughters. Now what makes this loving exchange of
place possible is the beautiful fluidity of the three
divine hypostases, who find their place in each other.
According to the doctrine of circumincession, as
defined by the Council of Florence, "the Father is
wholly in the Son and wholly in the Holy Spirit; the
Son wholly in the Father and wholly in the Holy
Spirit; the Holy Spirit wholly in the Father and wholly
in the Son".[32] In other words, the "place" of the
Father is the Son; the place of the Son is the Father.
The place of the Holy Spirit is Father and Son. Each
enfolds the others. Each person has his "centre" in
another or others. Father, Son, and Holy Spirit are
ecstatic persons: they are themselves by being outside
of themselves. Now it is this Trinitarian selflessness
which is manifested in Christ's human relations: he

wants to put himself where men are in their misery, not just statically alongside them, but dynamically, in revelation of the intra-Trinitarian ecstasy of love, taking over their burden from them, suffering not just like them but somehow in their place.[33]

Balthasar also brings out the Trinitarian depth to that vital theme of the New Testament: the *giving up* (*Dahingabe*) of the Son. In the first place, Jesus is given up by God the Father, who thereby shows his love for the world (cf. Rom. 8:32; John 3:16). This is a giving up of love, of infinite holiness, but it is a giving of the Son in a vulnerable human nature, a sending into a sinful world. And so there is an unholy "giving up" through the dramatic collision of self-giving Trinitarian freedom and selfish human freedom. Jesus is, therefore, "handed over", "delivered", "into the hands of men", to "the chief priests" and "the Gentiles" (*paradidotai, tradetur*, Mark 9:31; *paradothêsetai, paradôsousin, tradetur, tradent*, Mark 10:33; etc). In the actual drama of salvation history, the human instrument by whom Jesus is "given up" is the *traditor* Judas, who thus inaugurates a series of handings over of the Lord in his self-emptied weakness: from the Jews to the Romans, from Pilate to Herod and back again.

> It fits in with the New Testament theology of the *Verbum caro* and the idea of being in relation to other human beings which that implies that, in addition to the Father who gives up and the Son who gives himself up, there should be the third actor, the traitor who gives him up.[34]

But Jesus is not just passively given up. He lets himself be given up. In divine freedom he is eternally ready to be given up; in human freedom he actively gives himself up (cf. John 10:18). So he is both given-up Lamb (John 1:28) and self-giving Priest (cf. Heb. 3:14). The words of institution at the Last Supper show that his self-giving precedes any giving up by men.[35] The givenness of the Son in the flesh is perpetual in the Eucharist.

I have contrasted the holy giving up by the Father and the unholy giving up by sinful men. One vital dimension is, however, missing from this. In the Old Testament when God "gives up" someone, he is expressing his *wrath* (cf. 1 Sam. 24:5). Now this is not a passion, as if God were subject to fits of rage. God's wrath is the form his love takes when it encounters sin's resistance to love. The Trinitarian God is a consuming fire, his love a blazing furnace, not a bland fondness. God the Father is not, could not be, angry with his beloved Son, nor does he ever cease to love his creatures, but he is analogically angry with the self-destructive folly of their wickedness, that sin of the world which his Son is willing to shoulder. So, in letting himself be given up, the Son is abandoning himself to the impact of the Father's No to sin, to the fire of his love as it scorches human unlove. He stands at the crossfire between the Father's rejection of sin and sinful mankind's rejection of love. In that crossfire the Trinity is revealed as an eternal communion of love.

> But this gift of self is only an "act" in the sense of being a consent to be delivered. This has to be seen in a Trinitarian context. The whole judicial action is contained within the love of the Father who gives up (Jn. 3:16) and the love of the Son who lets himself be disposed of: within this bracket is found all the violence of the curse of the world's sin falling upon the Unique One who bears it (Gal. 3:13).[36]

The great mystery of the Cross is this: the Son's abandonment there by the Father is the supreme revelation of the consubstantial Trinity. Balthasar states as a self-evident axiom: "No one can be more abandoned by the Father than the Son, because no one knows and lives in such dependence on Him as the Son".[37] "Only God can go as far as extreme abandonment by God. He alone has the freedom needed to go that far".[38] What makes possible the Godforsakenness of Calvary is "the absolute distance, within the Trinity, between the hypostasis who gives away the Godhead and the One who receives it", a distance which the Hypostasis who proceeds from the Giver and Receiver as their mutual Gift [the Holy Spirit] both bridges and keeps open.[39]

The incarnate Son's experience in his human nature of the apparent absence of the Father manifests the real distinction of persons: the Son is not the Father; the Father is not the Son. But the ecstatic, devoted movement of the Son towards the Father, even in the midst of Godforsakenness, shows that he is the consubstantial Son, the One who loves the Father eternally in the unity of the Holy Spirit. Just as in the immanent life of the Trinity, so here in "economic" revelation, the Spirit brings about the highest unity in distinction of Father and Son. Even on Calvary, in the very Godforsakenness of the Son, the Spirit is revealed as the "bond of love".

> If the Spirit is the "Go-Between" of Father and Son, he is so supremely on the Cross, when he both shows and makes the greatest "separation" of the Two to be the manifestation of their supreme unity.[40]

Moreover, in Christ's Godforsakenness, the Trinity, the Three in One and One in Three, is revealed to us as loving and saving us.

> Here an abyss of mystery opens up. For there is, in fact, an infinite distinction in God between the begetting womb, the Father, and the begotten fruit,

the Son, although both in the Holy Spirit are only one God. Many theologians nowadays rightly say: it is precisely on the Cross that this difference is fully revealed; precisely there that the mystery of the divine Trinity is disclosed. The distance is so great – for, after all, everything in God is infinite – that all the estrangement and sin of the world has a place within it, that the Son can take it into his relationship with the Father, without the eternal mutual love of Father and Son in the Holy Spirit being injured or changed at all. Sin is, as it were, burnt up in the fire of this love, for "God", says Scripture, "is a consuming fire" that tolerates nothing impure in itself but burns it all up.

The incarnate Son loves the Father so much that he is ready to let the living fire of the fatherly love burn up the dross of sin that he bears. Alienation, the otherness of sin, is therefore replaced by the Trinitarian otherness of love. The children of wrath thereby become the children of God. Their situation has been objectively changed: their sinful distance from God has been transformed into a proximity of peace.

> The Son takes "estrangement upon himself and creates nearness": nearness to God and man because of the union of Father and Son maintained in the midst of all the darkness and dereliction. The "separation" experienced in bearing the world's guilt "was not an estrangement from the Father, for the Son constantly directs himself towards the Father in order to stand at the very centre of his mission".[41]

The apparent sign of separation of Father and Son is in fact a sign of supreme union.

The incarnate Son suffers and dies *pro nobis*, in our place, taking our place. He alone, the all-holy

God-Man, can do this for us. And yet he does not do it entirely without us. For what is sealed in his blood is the new and everlasting covenant, and covenants are bonds between two partners, in fact, a marriage. We see the Yes of the Bridegroom. Where is the Yes of the Bride? With Balthasar's help, I shall try to answer that question in the next chapter.

Balthasar on Godforsakenness: An Evaluation

Balthasar's presentation of Christ's dereliction is beautiful but very difficult. First, he seems to me to distinguish insufficiently between the *feeling* of abandonment and its *reality*. As Pope John Paul has said in his catechetical address on the cry of dereliction, "if Jesus feels abandoned by the Father, he knows however that that is not really so. He himself said: 'I and the Father are one' (John 10:30)".[42] I think it would be helpful to state more clearly that the Father's abandonment of the Son is not a spurning or rejection, but, as St Thomas says, his non-protection of the Son from his persecutors.[43] A link with the other modes of salvation would also be illuminating. Christ assumes Godforsakenness not for its own sake but in order to make satisfaction for human sin. To quote the Holy Father again, "if sin is separation from God, Jesus had to experience, in the crisis of his union with the Father, a suffering proportionate to that separation".[44]

The experience of Godforsakenness, according to Balthasar, is all-consuming, enveloping and penetrating the whole of Our Lord's soul, excluding, *at any level*, joy or beatitude. This runs counter to the Scholastic view that from his conception, even during his Passion, Jesus as man was *simul viator et comprehensor*,[45] at once pilgrim and beholder, sufferer and seer, enjoying the beatific vision of his Father,[46] and yet feeling a sorrow surpassing all the suffering endured or endurable by men in this present life.[47] St Thomas explains this by saying that Our Lord's human will to suffer for us prevented happiness flowing from the summit of his soul, where he looks on the face of his Father, down to its relatively lower slopes, where he is assailed by the storms of agony. Pope John Paul has reproduced this doctrine in his address:

> Dominant in his mind, Jesus has the clear vision of God and the certainty of his union with the Father. But in the sphere bordering the senses, and therefore more subject to the impressions, emotions and influences of the internal and external experiences of pain, Jesus' human soul is reduced to a wasteland, and he no longer feels the "presence" of the Father, but he undergoes the tragic experience of the most complete desolation . . . In the sphere of feelings and affection this sense of the absence and abandonment by God was the most acute pain for the soul of Jesus, who drew his strength and joy from union with the Father. This pain rendered more intense all the other sufferings. That lack of interior consolation was his greatest agony.[48]

Balthasar finds himself unable to accept the Scholastic picture of Christ's dereliction, at least as presented by such recent advocates as Johannes Stöhr and Bertrand de Margerie SJ.

> Any theology (including present-day echoes) which says that Christ on the Cross suffered only in the "lower" part of his soul, while the "peak of his [created] spirit" continued to enjoy the heavenly beatific vision, breaks the top off the drama of redemption. It does not see that the Son, as a

whole, takes on himself the situation of the sinful world that has turned away from God; indeed, by his absolute obedience he has "infiltrated" it and rendered it impotent. The Triune God is capable of more than pious theologians imagine. At the same time, it is absolutely true that this "dereliction" between Father and Son (made possible through their common Spirit) is a most extreme form of their mutual love and of God's Triune love for the world.[49]

He would prefer to develop Adrienne's intuitions about Christ having vision as "beholder" and faith as "pilgrim", a thesis apparently at odds with the traditional view that Christ as man knew the Father directly by a knowledge that is higher than faith, the knowledge that is in fact beatific (*scientia beata*). Balthasar and Adrienne try to get beyond the opposition of faith to sight. The Son as man does not like us "walk by faith", but he does have on earth "the form of vision most closely comparable to our faith"; (faith, in any case, as St Thomas Aquinas perceived, is itself a kind of seeing, has its own light). The absolute criterion is his mission: the Son "leaves behind" (*hinterlegt*), deposits in the hands of the Father, those possible perfections of his human nature which would obstruct his mission of obedience. If, therefore, in his "pilgrim" state, on the Cross, his vision is "dimmed" or "not used", this is in order to transform the death-black night of sinful man, whom he was sent to seek and to save.[50]

I should guess that St Thomas would reply to Balthasar's critique that the conjunction of happiness and agony in the soul of Christ is incredible only if joy invariably alleviates pain. Now such alleviation is precisely what Christ, in the Scholastic view, deliberately prevents from happening.[51] It is at least arguable that the greatest possible spiritual suffering is not so much the Godforsakenness of One who *hitherto* has enjoyed the vision of the Father but rather the feeling of God's absence in a soul that still, at some level, rests in his presence.[52] Before the Resurrection, Christ's vision of the Father is at the apex of his human soul and, therefore, above and beyond consciousness.[53] If, by his direct will, its beatifying influence is impeded, then surely it weighs upon him as an exquisite heightening and deepening of pain. A hint of what this coincidence of profound peace and acute anguish might mean is to be found in the great mystics, indeed, as Bertrand de Margerie has pointed out, in the experience of many ordinary men and women.[54] Could it not be, as the seventeenth century Dominican Louis de Chardon argued, that the one plenitude of grace in Our Lord's soul was the principle of both its unconquerable joy and its inconceivably immense sorrow?[55]

Two

Mary, the Mass and the Mysteries of March

5
Mary and the Mysteries of March

The mysteries of March meet in Mary, the Virgin Mother of God. At the Annunciation she says Yes to the Incarnation of God the Son in her womb. On Calvary she consents to the Sacrifice he offers for the sins of the world. When he rises in glory from the tomb, her *fiat* flows into a jubilation beyond words. Mary gives her undivided assent to the whole mission of Jesus, from Lady Day to Easter Day and to the ages of ages.

> At the beginning, at the very heart of the Incarnation event, stands Mary, the perfect Virgin, who "let it be done unto her", who was prepared to enter into a physical and spiritual motherly relationship with the person and also the whole work of her Son.[1]

For Balthasar, there can be no Christology without Trinitarian doctrine, but there can likewise be no Christology without Mariology, neither Incarnation nor Cross without the Virgin who said Yes. Adrienne von Speyr said to Balthasar a year or two after her conversion, "if [Mary] is taken away, all you are left with is an abstract Redeemer".[2] She knew from her own experience that the "Christ alone" (*solus Christus*) principle of Protestantism threatened to dehumanize Christ. There are no solitary stars in the human galaxy; every man "belongs to a constellation with his fellow men" (*einer mitmenschlichen Konstellation*)".[3] If it is "not good for a man to be alone" (cf. Gen. 2:18), it is not good for the God-Man to be alone.[4] The divine person of the Son is a "subsistent relation": being Son is "being towards the Father". Now when he becomes man, he enters the world of human relationships, sanctifying them, raising them, through his relational Trinitarian personality, to a dignity beyond compare. Jesus' relations with other human beings can never be routine, merely neutral or casual, least of all his relation with Mary, his Mother and Handmaid. As the history of the Reformed denominations proves, to sever the Son from the Mother in whose flesh and by whose faith he became man produces a Christology of unsustainable abstraction. And that is not all: a Maryless doctrine of Christ inevitably means a coldly impersonal or masculine picture of the Church. Catholics and Eastern Orthodox have always seen the Church personified in Mary, the Ever-Virgin Theotokos; the Church is "she", a person, a woman, Christ's Bride and our Mother. But, for Protestantism, the Church tends to be an "it" or a "he", not a surrounding maternal presence but an oppressive institution or a gang of interfering clergymen. In a collection of essays published nearly twenty years ago, commenting on Karl Barth's "jovially malicious" remark that he had never heard a Roman Catholic sermon on Mary on Swiss radio, Balthasar warned his fellow Catholics of the calamitous effects of their losing "the Marian principle".

Without Mariology Christianity threatens imperceptibly to become inhuman. The Church becomes functionalistic, soulless, a hectic enterprise without any point of rest, estranged from its true nature by the planners. And because, in this manly-masculine world, all that we have is one ideology replacing another, everything becomes polemical, critical, bitter, humourless, and ultimately boring, and people in their masses run away from such a Church.[5]

Mary's Yes at the Annunciation

The bond between Jesus and his Mother is spiritual as well as bodily. The idea that it could be merely biological is humanly as well as theologically unthinkable.[6] Mary "devotes herself totally as Handmaid of the Lord to the person and work of her Son",[7] in soul as well as body, and throughout the whole of her life. St Augustine, followed by St Leo, expresses the totality of this mothering by the adage that the Virgin conceived Jesus in her mind by faith before she conceived him in her womb.[8] Everything about Mary is Catholic, "according to the whole". Her consent to the Incarnation is wholehearted and wholepersoned, without reservation and engaging every fibre of her being.

The full consent of the Mother was already required at the time of the Incarnation of the Son . . . this Yes of Mary had to be a consent of total faith, without limit, without any restriction. For at least three reasons: first, because God, in becoming incarnate in the Virgin, does not violate his creature; secondly, because this Mother had to be capable of introducing her Son into the plenitude of Israel's religion, into perfect Abrahamic faith; thirdly, because the Incarnation of the Word requires precisely a flesh which itself welcomes him perfectly; in other words, because the faith of this Mother had to encompass her whole person, body and soul, it had to be an incarnate faith.[9]

In the Mariological section of the *Theodramatik,* Balthasar states as a principle: God "could not use force on his free creation".[10] The Father does not inflict salvation, does not impose the Saviour-Son. He turns to Mary, appeals to her will, waits for her reply. Our God, as Julian of Norwich liked to say, is a *courteous* Lord.[11] So Mary is not "passively used by God but helps in free faith and obedience, to effect the salvation of men".[12] She cooperates, in a humble, handmaidenly way, with the saving work of the Trinity.

For Hans Urs von Balthasar and Adrienne von Speyr, Marian consent is the "fundamental attitude" of all Christian faith and love, of contemplative prayer and active service, "the original vow, out of which arises every form of definitive Christian commitment to God and in God".[13] If we want to know what it means to know and love and follow Jesus in the Church, then we must turn in loving devotion to Mary, his Mother and ours. By contrast with all the aggressively masculine, Promethean pictures of what it is to be a Christian, Hans Urs and Adrienne refer us to the heart of the matter, to the immaculate heart of the Mother. There, for example, is to be found the secret of prayer.[14] Praising God in the Magnificat, contemplating Jesus in her heart, prayerfully awaiting the Spirit with the apostles, Mary is the supreme model in prayer as she is in everything else that is Christian. To be Mary is to be prayer.[15]

Mary's Yes is virginal, the assent of a woman who looks to God's omnipotence alone for new life and fruitfulness. The virginity of her body is the exact sacrament of her poverty of spirit, her unresisting readiness to receive what God gives her.

Mary's life must be regarded as the prototype of what the *Ars Dei* can fashion from a human material which puts up no resistance to him. It is a feminine life which, in any case more than masculine life, awaits being shaped by the man, the Bridegroom, Christ, and God. It is a virginal life which desires no other formative principle but God and the fruit which God gives it to bear, to give birth to, to nourish and to rear. It is at the same time a maternal and a bridal life whose power of surrender reaches from the physical to the highest spiritual level. In all this it is simply a life that lets God dispose of it as he will.[17]

Mary's virginal Yes is representative. She gives her consent to the Incarnation on behalf of all Israel. She sums up and fulfils but then surpasses all the faith and obedience of her people since Abraham. Israel's faith was constantly failing, regularly flawed by hesitation, doubt, even flagrant infidelity. Here at last, by the grace of the Immaculate Conception, is the all-pure Daughter of Zion, unreservedly ready to give herself to God.

God looked on "his servant in her lowliness" and did in her the "great things" he promised to "Abraham and his seed", as Mary herself says in her hymn to grace. But this means that her Yes to the angel summed up and surpassed all the faith and all the obedience of the Old Testament from Abraham onwards. It means, too, that it integrated the Old Covenant with the New, Judaism with the Church.[18]

Mary is Israel in person, Israel at its most perfect and beautiful, the Old Testament fulfilled in the New.

It is not only Israel that Mary represents by her Yes. At the Annunciation she gives her assent on behalf of all mankind, indeed of all creation. To see how this is so, we must follow Balthasar in regarding revelation as a nuptial mystery. Many of the Church Fathers speak of the hypostatic union as a marriage (*connu-bium*) of the divine and human natures. In the earliest expressions of this, Mary's womb is seen as the "bridal chamber" in which the Son of God espouses human nature. Eventually, however, the tradition begins to see that she is more than the venue of the nuptials.

> Mary cannot be the impersonal "place" where the marriage bond of the two natures is tied. God does not do violence to his creature, especially not to the woman who represents his covenant. He treats her with respect as a person, as embodying that human nature which his Word and Son will assume and, in that sense, as endowed with a coresponsibility.[19]

Since the Incarnation is not an invasion but a wedding, God wants mankind gladly to say "I will", to give him its nature freely by a responsive and spousal love. Mary fulfils that role for us all at the Annunciation. Balthasar cherishes St Thomas' way of saying it:

> In order to show that there is a certain spiritual wedlock (*matrimonium*) between the Son of God and human nature, in the Annunciation the Virgin's consent was besought in lieu of that of the entire human nature.[20]

In other words, the marriage of divinity and humanity in the one person of Christ does not derive its matrimonial character exclusively from the side of the Bridegroom-Son. No, says Balthasar, it is "a real two-sided mystery of love through the bridal consent of Mary acting for all the rest of created flesh".[21]

It is precisely as a woman, because she is a woman, that Mary can represent all humanity at the Incarnation. Woman by nature is receptive, responsive, reflective: the womb that receives the seed of man, the answer to his word, the face that shines back its love to him.[22] Now Balthasar argues that, in Old and New Testaments, the relation between God and his creatures is presented in the light of this nuptial mystery. God in his transcendence, as the primary actor and initiator, is analogically male with regard to the creature; the creature in its dependence on God is open and receptive, *capax Dei*, and therefore, in a certain sense, feminine.[23] It is true, says Balthasar, that modern physiology has demonstrated that, in the act of generation, the female contribution is as active as the male.

> It is nonetheless undeniable that the woman is the one who receives and that it is the man who gives. Conclusion: receiving, consenting, accepting, letting happen can be an attitude no less active and creative than that of giving, fashioning, imposing. And if in the Incarnation the part of man is taken by God, who is essentially the Giver, indeed the Imposer, the part of woman, who as a creature accepts the divine gift, is far from being passive. Let us say rather that this assent is the highest and most fruitful of human activities – in Pauline terms, faith is required more fundamentally than works.[24]

Woman is the classic creature. It is supremely fitting, therefore, that a woman on her own, a virgin in fact, should have represented creation in consenting to the Incarnation. For the Yes asked of her is *ein geschehenlassendes Ja*, a *fiat*, a letting-it-be-done-in-her according to God's will. Men are men, but at that great moment Man was a woman.[25]

Incarnation, Cross, and Immaculate Conception

On the Solemnity of the Immaculate Conception the Church reads the Annunciation gospel. The collect of the day explains why: by preserving the Blessed Virgin from all stain of original sin, God the Father is preparing a "worthy dwelling-place" for his Son. Through the grace that fills her from the first moment of her existence, Our Lady is enabled, at the Annunciation, to welcome God's Son into her womb with a faith that is boundless and uncalculating, "infinitely at the disposal of the Infinite".[26] Someone affected by original sin "could not realize such an ingenuous openness".[27] So, through what Catholic theology calls the "pre-redemption" of his Mother, God the Son has "so arranged it that her assent should be immaculate, unweakened in childlike trust".[28]

Mary Immaculate personifies the Catholic "both/and", according to which God and his creatures, in dependence on God, cooperate in nature and grace. Her *fiat* is God's achievement in her, the flowering of the grace which has filled her soul from her conception, but it is also truly hers – fully hers *because* firstly his.

> Coming from God, this Yes is the highest grace; but coming from man, it is also the highest achievement made possible by grace: unconditional, definitive self-surrender.[29]

Grace makes possible self-surrender, and engraced self-surrender makes possible cooperation. Through pre-redemptive grace, Mary's assent is "disencumbered from the beginning . . . so that the earthly finite . . . offers no obstacle to the indwelling of God".[30] No sinful self obtrudes. By grace she is transparent to grace, and so, as Hopkins puts it, lets "all God's glory through".[31]

> In assenting, she renounces herself, makes herself nothing, in order to let God alone become active in her. She makes all the potentialities which constitute her nature accessible to his action, without her being able or wishing to overlook anything. She resolves to let God alone work; and yet, precisely by virtue of this resolution, she becomes cooperative . . . In renouncing all her potentialities, she obtains their fulfilment beyond all expectation: cooperative in body, she becomes the Mother of the Lord; cooperative in spirit, she becomes his Handmaid and his Bride.[32]

A wonderful circle of grace joins the Immaculate Conception of the Mother with the Incarnation and Cross of the Son. In time, the Immaculate Conception comes first, but it is made possible by the great events to which it is the prelude. Its final cause is Mary's divine motherhood (she is immaculately conceived in order to prepare her to be Mother of God), and its meritorious cause is the Sacrifice on Calvary (it is by the power of Christ's redeeming death that Mary is preserved from all stain of original sin). This suggests a further bond between the obedience of Mary and the obedience of Jesus. The Yes of Mary makes possible the Yes of Jesus (for without her he would not have a human nature and thus a human will with which to obey the Father), but it is also true that the Yes of Jesus makes possible the Yes of Mary (for it is by the grace of his Cross that Mary's faith is immaculate and unbounded). The Mother's obedience is an anticipated participation in the obedience of the Son.[33] Her freely given assent to the Incarnation is prepared for in advance by the "retroactive" application of the merits of Christ. Through the work of the Holy Spirit, Mary's

Yes is "enclosed in the Son's Yes to the Father and His sending into the world".[34]

Mary's Yes to the Disconcerting Ministry of her Son

> It is essential to this infinite flexibility of Marian consent that time and again it is led over and beyond its own understanding and has to assent to things which generally seem not to lie within the limits of the humanly possible, conceivable, tolerable, suitable . . . More and more is demanded of Mary's understanding, and in this her readiness is extended to be more and more limitless and unresisting. This shows Mary absolutely to be the believer whom the Lord counts blessed (cf. Luke 1:45; 11:28; John 20:29).[35]

Mary's "infinite flexibility" shows itself in her courageous readiness to go into the unknown, giving herself up more and more to what she does not fully understand. Here she is truly the model for our faith: not fully comprehending, yet believing and saying Yes.

> Mary is infinitely at the disposal of the Infinite. She is absolutely ready for everything, for a great deal more, therefore, than she can know, imagine or begin to suspect.[36]

For example, St Luke tells us that when Our Lady and St Joseph find the boy Jesus in the Temple, they do not understand his words about having to be in the Father's house (cf. 2:50). And yet the very next verse says that "his Mother kept all these things in her heart" (v.51). She treasures by the prayer of faith what she cannot exhaustively understand. She knows that

70

her Son, in his origin and his destiny, is unique, but she does not try to resolve the enigma of his life. Her pondering is contemplation not calculation. She looks with eyes of love on her mysterious Son, but she does not insist on knowing everything in advance. And in this way she conforms herself to him.

> Jesus does not anticipate in his mind the destiny that is come; he just lets himself be guided, day by day, by the Father. His Mother likewise does not anticipate anything of what is to come. One of the features of her faith (which is the fulfilment of Abraham's) is constantly to accept only what God decrees.[37]

Mary is called to follow Jesus into the dark: "the night of the senses and of the spirit, faith reduced to utter nakedness". Balthasar here is close in spirit to the tender yet down-to-earth Mariology of St Thérèse, who, in the very last poem she wrote ("Why I love you, O Mary"), shows Our Lady living out her immaculate all-holiness, not in luminous raptures, but in the dark and humble way of faith. Pope John Paul, too, in *Redemptoris Mater*, has spoken of Mary's faith, for the love of Jesus, entering the night.[38]

In the gospels, after Bethlehem, whenever the Son meets his Mother, he appears to distance himself from her: at the age of twelve, he leaves her, without explanation, to spend three days in his Father's house (Lk. 2:41–51); at Cana, he says, "O woman, what have you to do with me?" (Jn. 2:4); on one occasion, in the middle of his public ministry, she is left standing at the door and hears him asking: "Who is my mother, and who are my brethren? . . . Whoever does the will of my Father in heaven is my brother, and sister, and mother" (Matt. 12:46–50); when a woman acclaims the womb that bore him, Jesus immediately replies: "Blessed rather are those who hear the word of God

71

and keep it" (Lk. 11:27–28); finally, at the Cross, he gives her a new son, a disciple in place of the Master, a mere man in place of true God (cf. Jn. 19:26).

Balthasar describes these episodes as "turnings away" (*Zurückweisungen*) of the Mother by the Son.[39] Far from placing any kind of question mark by the Church's devotion to the Mother of God, they furnish it with a most powerful support. Take, for example, the two occasions where the Lord appears to be pointing beyond the merely physical fact of motherhood: "Whoever does the will of my Father . . . is my Mother"; "Blessed rather are those who hear the word of God and keep it". Here Jesus opens up to us the immaculate heart of Mary. He shows us that motherhood is not just biological: Mary is his Mother in the whole of her person, in soul as well as body, by her faith as well as in her flesh. Then again, if Jesus removes himself from her, it is not out of cruelty. On the contrary, he is inviting her to join him, even more closely, in his mission of love. He is abandoning her as he will be abandoned by the Father on the Cross. And in both cases, the abandonment, paradoxically, reveals the perfect loving union of Abandoner and Abandoned.[40]

> This form of union was necessary so that Mary – who henceforth will form the centre of the Church – may know by experience the mystery of Redemption and can transmit it to her new children. Specifically Christian humility cannot be learnt except by formal and repeated humiliations. Just as Christ humbled himself as far as the Cross so he could exercise the mission of the Father, so he humbles his Mother and confers her ecclesial mission by a final humiliation.[41]

By these mysterious distancings, Jesus transforms his Mother's Yes from being the perfect faith of Israel to being the crucified faith of the Church, a faith which does more than "hope against hope", as Abraham did, but collaborates with the Redeemer by going into dark Godforsakenness with him. Just as Mary once initiated the child Jesus into the tradition of his people, so now he teaches her the demands of his mission and of his Church's share in it.

> The "Yes" of the Handmaid remains the interior form of all the events that follow, however unexpected or shocking. This imperturbable Yes, which she gives through all the nights and incomprehensions, is the basis of what can be called collaboration, Marian and ecclesial coredemption.[42]

In her night, Mary's faith is enlarged, becomes truly Catholic. When Jesus says, in her hearing, "Whoever does the will of my Father in heaven is . . . my mother", he is "asking her to give up her maternal prerogative for the sake of a certain universality".[43] He is inviting Mary to let the Church participate in her motherhood of faith and obedience. The God-Man wants us to conceive him by faith and give birth to him in charity, to mother him into our lives by obedience to his Father. In making room for others in her motherly faith, Mary shows herself to be the concrete embodiment of what and who the Church is: the faith of the Church is quite simply a continuation of Mary's, the one who first believed. In this readiness to let all the faithful believe with and in her, Our Lady is the very personification of Catholicity. She is the primal believer, our motherly forerunner in faith, in a sense the very path of faith we tread in following Jesus.

> Mary's *fiat* . . . is a nuptial womb . . . where the Son of God can not only take existence but also found a truly universal Church.[44]

This relation between Mary and the Church is not one of merely exterior resemblance. Balthasar is not just saying that what Our Lady once did for Christ, the Church now does for his members, or for him in his members. No, Our Lady actually cooperates in the birth and growth of the Church's sons and daughters. It is through the Queen of Heaven's motherly love and prayers that the Church on earth fulfils her motherly role. Mary mothers the Church into mothering.

Mary's Yes to the Cross

Like her consent to the Incarnation, Mary's faithful Yes to her Son's Sacrifice on the Cross is feminine, at one and the same time virginal, motherly, bridal, representative. It is a *fiat*, a "letting it be done" of womanly and handmaidenly humility, which accepts its distance from the male and priestly self-oblation of the God-Man.

> This is the only way the New Eve can be the helpmate of the New Adam. He bears the guilt of all mankind before the Father . . . He makes room for the very different contribution of his Mother. What she has to do is painfully to let his suffering happen, by her own suffering, letting his suffering happen in her. Mary's *fiat* beneath the Cross is the archetypal *fiat* for all faith in the Church, not least in the Eucharist . . . [45]

In the Holy Spirit, who has filled her from her conception, and who overshadowed her at the Incarnation, Mary on Calvary gives the Son back to the Father, or rather she lets the Son return to the Father. And in that gesture she is the model for the faith of the Church and the individual Christian.

74

The more seriously Christians take this letting-it-happen-in-me for themselves and their whole life of following Jesus, the more Marian is their baptismal faith. But because of that they are also linked with Mary's gesture of giving back her Son, from the beginning as far as the Cross, to the Father in the Holy Spirit. The Son has to do all the work that the Father wants him to do, and so into that work he fits Mary and all mankind.[46]

In the Patristic eyes of Balthasar, the Lady who stands by the Cross is indistinguishably both Mary and the Church. When, like Vatican II, he says that Mary is the Church's "type" or "model", he means much more than that she is a poetic symbol of the Church. In an important sense, she *is* the Church, a *Realsymbol*, as the Germans say, a symbol which contains the very thing it symbolizes. Precisely as the historical person she is, the Blessed Virgin is the Church's embodiment and personification, the "concrete universal (*universale concretum*) of the Church as Jesus is of divine sonship".[47] By her virginal mothering of Christ, she is the first person to live in the bodily, believing relationship to him to which his whole Church is predestined.

At the foot of the Cross Mary personifies the Church as described by St Paul: "without spot or wrinkle or any such thing . . . holy and without blemish" (cf. Eph. 5:27). Through the sanctifying grace of her Son, received at the first moment of her conception, she is "the only member of the real pilgrim Church to correspond fully to the ecclesial attribute 'immaculate'".[48] Now, as we have seen, Mary is immaculate through the anticipated merits of Christ. At the foot of the Cross she stands as already redeemed through the Cross. In other words, as Adrienne points out, "pre-redemption" makes "co-redemption" possible. It is only by the grace of the

Redeemer, given her from her beginning, that she can cooperate with him. "She is not pre-redeemed through co-redemption, but through pre-redemption she becomes Co-Redemptrix".[49] Our Lady does not in any sense redeem herself, nor on Calvary does she merit the grace to be pre-redeemed. No, through her Son's grace, bestowed in advance, she is empowered to say Yes, in a humble and handmaidenly way, to the Sacrifice from which all grace flows.

It is on Calvary that the bridal aspect of Mary's faith becomes most evident. "Mary begins by being the Mother, but at the Cross she finishes by becoming Bride, the quintessence of the Church".[50] She somehow embodies the Church as the cherished spouse for whom Christ gives himself up on the Cross (cf. Eph. 5:25f.). Balthasar treats this idea of Mary as "Bride of the Word" (*Sponsa Verbi*) with immense reverence and delicacy. It is Mary's spiritual consent to the Sacrifice that is analogically bridal. She is Bride as the representative, the living summation, of the humankind for whom Jesus lays down his life. She is Bride as New Eve, helpmate of the New Adam. On the Cross the Head and Bridegroom gives himself up Eucharistically for love of the Church, and the Church in Mary accepts the gift. Jesus does not want the Church's faith to be given simply *post factum*. He wants a "simultaneous, instantaneous consent, so that his Sacrifice might be truly total: inseparably, the Sacrifice of the Head and the members".[51] Even in the utter loneliness and dereliction of Calvary, forsaken by his Father, deserted by all but one of his disciples, Jesus does not want "to act alone, without the accompaniment of his Church".[52]

Mary and John

On Golgotha, Mary is both Church and Mother of the Church. Together with St John she is the "first cell of the community founded by the Crucified Son".[53] But then, by his last will and testament, she becomes Mother of John and in him of all Christians, Mother of the Church.[54]

To appreciate fully what the relationship of Mary and John signifies for Balthasar, we must consider once more his concept of "the Christological Constellation". The eternal Son of the Father became a man of a particular time and place, and so entered into concrete historical relationships, a whole "constellation" of kinship and friendship. His central place is secure, but he shines inseparably from other stars.

> It is impossible to detach Jesus from the human group which forms a totality with him, even though this statement does not take away anything from his sovereign position. As soon as one abstracts him (and the doctrine about him, Christology) from it, he becomes a desperately abstract figure, even if the Trinitarian context is still there.[55]

In the middle of the Christological Constellation, immediately round Jesus himself, are his Blessed Mother and his apostles, pre-eminently Peter, the rock on which he builds his Church, and John, the disciple whom he specially loves, the evangelist who is his "most profound expositor", the virgin custodian of his Virgin Mother.[56] "These figures belong . . . to the constellation of Jesus and are consequently *integral parts of Christology*".[57] They are also, argues Balthasar, intrinsic to ecclesiology. For the Lord has made them "types", "real symbols", of his Church, "mediatory figures" by which "the 'form of Christ' (Gal. 4:19) is imprinted upon the whole People of God".[58]

77

This typological ecclesiology is thought out with philosophical and sacramental realism. In Christ the universal is concrete and personal, the particular given general scope. Through the animating operation of the Holy Spirit the incarnate Son's historical, human relations are perpetuated in his Mystical Body as complementary dimensions of her being and function. Mary, the Virgin Theotokos, by her faith and loving accord, is the perfect personal realization of the *Ecclesia Immaculata*; Peter, who speaks and acts in his successors, the Roman Pontiffs, represents the male, office-bearing part of the Church; and John, apostle-priest of Jesus yet adoptive son of Mary, is the link between the two.

For Balthasar, Our Lord's words from the Cross to Mary and John "in a way constitute the Church's foundation document".[59] By bequeathing her to John, Jesus unites the heavenly Church, perfected in advance, with the still struggling, earthly Church. In other words, the visibly organized pilgrim Church on earth, in all its imperfection, has been entrusted by its Head to care for and protect "the purity and sanctity of the original – the ideal – Church".[60] John's mission is to be the link between Mary and Peter and thus between the Church as holy and immaculate, and the Church as hierarchical and infallible, between the whole Church, which, even as distinct from Christ, is greater than its members and surrounds them as a motherly presence, and that sacramentally consecrated portion, which is masculine and fatherly, the office of unity in the truth.[61] John represents the official side of the Church, but in a special form – as uniting office and love.[62] On Calvary John is the vicar of the absent Peter; he undertakes, in lieu of the primate, to cherish and guard Holy Mother Mary and thus Holy Mother Church, the Church as a whole, the Church as holy.[63] John is the one whom Jesus specially loves, and yet it is of Peter that the "greater love" is asked (cf. John 21:15). The Rock, fragile in himself, yet in Christ indestructible, loves much because he has been forgiven much. He can strengthen his brethren, because he has himself been strengthened. Jesus leads him, through his tears, to a John-like love, "so that in him the unity Christ established between office and love can survive unto death (21:19)"[64].

The figures of Mary and John at the Cross have something to teach every Christian, but they have a special significance for those who follow Jesus in the way of the evangelical counsels, by poverty, celibacy, and obedience.

> The Mary-John community, established in the Petrine Church, has its origin in the Cross, emanates from it and always returns to it. It is in the obedience of the Cross and in the poverty of the Cross that it is entered. It is also a virginal community. This threefold renunciation lives henceforth in the heart of the Church as her secretly life-giving nucleus, healing the wounds of Church and world by leading them back to the source of all salvation and healing.[65]

For the members of the secular institute founded by Balthasar and Adrienne, the Community of St John, Mary, John, and Peter define their life. The model for the priest is John in his closeness to the Lord's Eucharistic Sacrifice of his life; for the layman engaged in a secular profession, it is John's vocation to "remain" in the world (cf. John 21:11f.); for the laywoman, it is Mary in her virginal openness to God. All three branches abide gratefully in one fold under Peter's successor.

Balthasar's "constellational ecclesiology" sheds light on many of the most difficult questions in the Church today. For example, it places the necessary maleness of the ministerial priesthood in its proper perspective. Apostles like Peter and John, followed by those who share their ministry as bishops and priests, act in the person of Christ, but they most certainly are not Christ. Peter would rather be crucified upside down than be confused with the Master. By the grace of ordination, these weak and sometimes foolish males are simply icons, sacramental signs and instruments, of Christ the Bridegroom-Priest. His are the words they speak in consecrating, his the forgiveness when they absolve. For the sake of their brethren, the office-bearers represent, as a portrait represents its subject, the Son of God made man and male. The Blessed Virgin is and does something far greater. She is not a priest as the apostles are, for she does not portray someone else. She just *is* the Mother of God, the one who in faith and love gave flesh and blood to God the Son, and she *is* the Church, Holy Church's personal embodiment as immaculate Bride. The Church as a whole is feminine, open to receive the life and truth of her Head; the male hierarchy, by contrast, is only one part, with the humble vocation to serve the feminine Marian whole. The Church, Balthasar insists, existed in a woman before a single man had been called to be an apostle: "In Mary the Church already has physical existence before it is organized in Peter".[66] Mary, not Peter or John, is "first Church". It was she who first believed and so made possible, on the human level, the mystery of the Incarnation. On Easter Day – at least as far as Ignatius, Adrienne, and Balthasar are concerned – Our Lady was the first to see the Son in the glory of his risen body.[67] And it is she who, when her earthly course was finished, was the first human person to share fully in that glory in body as well as soul, brilliant sign of hope for her pilgrim children. Our Lady is primate in a way that no prelate could ever be.

Being laid in the hands of Mary at his birth and after his death is more central than being laid in the hands of office, and the presupposition of the latter. Before male office makes its appearance in the Church, the Church as woman and helpmate is on the scene . . . The Marian takes precedence over the liturgical, because the incarnate Word was first entrusted to the care of His Mother at his Incarnation and birth before being later placed in the care of the Church in the official and institutional sense.[68]

The centre of the Church is not a clergyman, but a laywoman, Our Blessed Lady. Not all of us are called to be priest or bishop or Pope, but every Christian is meant to be like Mary in her faith and to know and love her as Mother.

This femininity of the Church is all-embracing, whereas the official service-role performed by the apostles and their male successors is merely a function within this all-embracing dimension.[69]

The classical Byzantine icon of Pentecost shows this beautifully. Peter is there with his keys, so is John, but the praying heart of the apostolic Church is Mary.

6
THE MASS AND THE
MYSTERIES OF MARCH

Holy Mass is an *anamnesis* of Our Lord's whole temporal history – of his Death and Resurrection, above all, but also, in an important sense, of his Incarnation.[1] Even on Holy Thursday evening, as the priest carries the Blessed Sacrament to the altar of repose, the Church does not forget Lady Day or Christmas Day.

> *Nobis datus, nobis natus*
> *Ex intacta Virgine . . .*
> Given for us, for us descending
> Of a Virgin to proceed . . .

The body received in Holy Communion is none other than the "true body born of the Virgin Mary" (*Ave verum Corpus natum de Maria virgine*), the body in which the Son was crucified (*vere passum, immolatum in cruce pro homine*), the body in which he gloriously arose, the body in which he will come again on the Last Day. Adrienne von Speyr was haunted by the Eucharist's debt to the Incarnation and so to the Mother of God.

> Whenever he now gives men his Body, his flesh and blood, in the Eucharist, it is the Body conceived and carried, formed and nourished, by his Mother, which she conceived by the Holy Spirit, enabling [the Son] to become man . . . It is impossible for this

82

unity in the flesh between Mother and Son ever to be broken. The Eucharist does not do away with it. That is why it is always the commemoration of the Mother's consent and of her bearing of the Son, because traces of her are always in his flesh.[2]

Early in 1942, Balthasar noted how, whenever Adrienne went into a church, she first of all instinctively greeted the Mother of God. "Even in the altar she sees and feels the Mother".[3] Moreover, she believed that Our Lady's disposition at the Annunciation is the model for every communicant at the altar. No one knows better than the Virgin Mother how to receive the Son. For at the Incarnation she welcomed him into her heart and into her womb with faith and love beyond compare. And now, every time we receive Jesus in Holy Communion, his Mother and ours stands nearby to help us, to bring to completeness what we do so brokenly. Balthasar made this idea his own. I can think of no theology that more decisively exorcizes Jansenist guilt about unworthy reception.

> We do not know whether Mary ever communicated at a celebration of the Eucharist. But she knows better than any saint or sinner what it means perfectly to receive the Son into oneself. She stands, as it were, behind every Holy Communion, as the *Ecclesia Immaculata*, bringing to perfection what we accomplish imperfectly.[4]

Balthasar and Adrienne also detect a Eucharistic typology in the second of the joyful mysteries, Mary's journey into Judaea, with Jesus in her womb.

> This attitude of letting himself be born and driven will be perfected in the Eucharist: here the Son will hand himself over to both the holy and the unholy spirit of the Church in order to stand at the disposal

of men who are not ready to let themselves be
determined by his grace, by his attitude of obedience. Now as a child, later on as a man, and finally
as a Host, the Son will let himself be borne about as
a thing that one can dispose of – and this is he who
bears the sin of the world and, therefore, the world
itself.[5]

One and the same Word incarnate, one and the same
love that lets itself be carried: in the womb by
gentleness, to the Cross by violence, in the Host by
the good and the not so good.

The Mass and the Last Supper

The Mass is itself one of the Mysteries of March, a gift
from the Lord on the first Holy Thursday. According
to Balthasar, the Last Supper is an anticipation of the
Cross.[6] Before he is passively handed over to his
violent death, Jesus actively hands himself as food to
his disciples, his flesh as "given", his blood as
"shed". He disposes, in advance of his being-
disposed-of in the Passion.

> The Son thanks the Father (*eucharistein*, *eulogein*) for
> allowing him to be disposed of in such a way that
> from it there flows both the highest revelation of
> divine love (its glorification) and the salvation of
> men.[7]

Behind the human and historical passivity and
activity of the Cross and its anticipation in the Supper,
somehow disclosed by it, is a divine and eternal giving
and readiness to be given. For the One who, as man,
"immortal food supplying, gives himself with his
own hand" is the consubstantial Son given, out of
love for the world, by God the Father (cf. John 3:16).[8]

The Last Supper is not a mere symbol, a kind of acted parable to show the spirit in which Jesus is to suffer. It is an act of the *Verbum caro*, in which flesh-blood and spirit-life (cf. John 6:52–57, 63) coincide. The washing of feet may be symbol, but the Supper is real sacramental anticipation.

> The interior attitude (symbolized by the washing of feet) finally becomes actuality in the self-distribution which anticipates and inaugurates the Passion.[9]

The Mass and the Cross

According to the teaching of the Council of Trent, in the Eucharist Christ's bloody Sacrifice on Calvary is made really present (*repraesentaretur*) and offered, in an unbloody way, through the ministry of priests.[10] Christ is the principal offerer and offering:[11] as St Augustine says, *Ipse offerens, ipse et oblatio*.[12] And the Church, Christ's beloved Bride, is co-offerer. On the night he was betrayed, the Bridegroom bequeathed his Sacrifice for her to offer, through her priests, under visible signs.[13] The Sacrifice is one and the same; only the manner of offering is different.

The first thing Balthasar wants to say about the Church's Eucharistic offering of Christ's Sacrifice is that it is a grace.

> Jesus hands over his Sacrifice at the Last Supper to his disciples in order that they may perform it in imitation . . . He himself passes from his active life to the passivity of suffering, of being overtaxed, in which one can no longer be active oneself but must suffer whatever happens. And thus he can hand over to his disciples the active aspect of his readiness for God: he gives his Sacrifice to them so that

they may have something to offer to God . . . Yes, [the Mass] is a Sacrifice: it is Christ's Sacrifice which he places into the hands of the Church so that she in turn has something to offer to the Father: the only thing of value, the Sacrifice of Christ.[14]

Even as actively offering, the Church as a whole is bridal in the sense that the Sacrifice is a gift femininely received from the Bridegroom. On the Cross Christ offered himself in sacrifice to the Father for us. In the Eucharist the Church, his Body and Bride, consents to and ratifies that oblation, "[wills] the death in an ecclesial and feminine way".[15] The model for this Eucharistic attitude of the Church, indeed its highest and holiest realization, is Mary's Yes at the foot of the Cross. From this Balthasar argues that Mariology can make an invaluable contribution to Eucharistic theology.

I believe that the expression "the Sacrifice of the Mass" will remain obscure unless we have met the woman who stands in the shadow of the Cross, who is both the Mother of the Crucified and the icon of the Church. She is present when the Son gives himself; she cannot intervene. But she is far from being passive. A superhuman action is demanded of her: to consent to the sacrifice of this man who is the Son of God, but also her own. She would prefer a thousand times over to be tortured in his place. But that is not what is required of her. She has only to consent. Actively, she has to let herself be dispossessed. She has to repeat her initial Yes to the very end, but this end was included virtually in the first *élan*. This acquiescing of the Mother is the original form, reserved to the pure creature, of participation in the sacrifice of Christ.[16]

The Eucharistic action of the Church as a whole is "a

Marian letting oneself be taken into Jesus' availability to the Father's will".[17] The active indicative *offerimus* is made possible by the petitionary subjunctive *fiat*.

Mary on Calvary is not a priestess; René Laurentin proved long ago that that idea had no foundation in Scripture or Tradition.[18] As we saw earlier, the mission of the Mother of God is immeasurably greater than that of any apostle or cleric. Our Lady's role is to say a "Yes that lets it happen" (*ein geschehenlassendes Ja*), that peculiarly feminine word of assent, apparently passive yet the most fruitful act of which any human person is capable. She is not a mediator like him but under, in and through him. On the Cross, the divine person of the Bridegroom-Priest, as man and male, offers himself to the Father in atonement for the whole world's sin. The human person of the Virgin Mother, as woman and embodiment of the Church immaculate, humbly lets herself be counted among sinful humanity, while at the same time giving the consent of which it is incapable.[19] Applying this to the Eucharist, we can see that Mary is the model, not of the celebrating priesthood, but of the whole worshipping Church, a real symbol of the common, not the ministerial, priesthood.[20] Ministerial priests, the Johns and Peters, are simply the sacramental signs and instruments of the chief Offerer, the Eternal High Priest. They are the male hands through which the female Body unbloodily offers the bloody Sacrifice of the Head. In the first place, as the Church has always taught, they represent Christ as an icon represents its subject, as an actor represents a character. They act in his person. This is an awesome but ultimately humiliating mission, for they are shown up by the part they play. Mary's immaculate Yes, by contrast, is not representative in the iconic or mimetic sense. In her there is no gap between actor and part, only a perfect coincidence of objective and subjective holiness.

87

Once again we must remember that the Marian takes precedence over the liturgical, because the incarnate Word was first entrusted to the care of his Mother in his Incarnation and Nativity before being later placed in the care of the Church in the official and institutional sense.[21]

Only in the light of the Virgin Theotokos can we understand why the necessary maleness of the ministerial priesthood does not in any way imply the inferiority of woman. True, the highest elevation of human nature (in the divine Word) took place in the male sex, but the supreme exaltation of the human person took place in the female (in Mary, the Mother of God).[22] The impossibility of women's ordination derives from the incomparable dignity of woman in the sexual order of creation and in the supernatural order of redemption and the Church. "The woman who would strive for the male role in the Church thus strives for something 'less' and denies the 'more' which she is".[23]

The Mass and the Trinity

The Eucharist has its presupposition in the Trinity. In the inner life of the Godhead, the divine essence which the Son eternally receives from the Father he offers back to him in gratitude, in love, in the Holy Spirit.[24] The Son is thanksgiving in his very person, "the Father's substantial Eucharist".[25] Of course, since Jesus is true man as well as true God, he is not Eucharist in this Trinitarian sense alone. His eternal thankful return of his divinity to the Father is incarnated in the surrender of his human body and soul, in the Holy Spirit, to the Father. As God from eternity, and as man from the Virgin's womb, the Son's love is grateful and self-giving. In his divinity, with regard to the generating Father, he is Eucharist in the sense of eternal gratitude. In his humanity, with regard to his brethren, he is Eucharist in the sense of a love that wants to distribute itself, a body ready to be broken, blood to be poured out, a heart to be wounded. And the two movements are one. In offering his body for us, in giving his body to us, the thankful Son fulfils his Father's will that we be drawn into the life of the Blessed Trinity. "As the living Father sent me, and I live because of the Father, so he who eats me will live because of me" (John 6:57).

It is important to realize that Jesus' grateful self-oblation as man is not just spiritual. He gives his human All to the Father for us, his material body as well as his spiritual soul. He pours out his life-blood, his whole living substance (cf. John 10:17ff.).[26] Bearing the crushing burden of the world's sin, plunged into Godforsakenness, scourged, crowned with thorns, and nailed to the tree, the Son says "I thank thee, Father", offering up his body, thereby making the supreme act of religion, the glorification of the Father, thanksgiving and sacrifice in one.

The Mass and the Resurrection

The gift which Our Lord on the Cross made of his whole self to us and his Father has never been withdrawn. In Heaven, in his glorified manhood, at the Father's right hand, he stands for ever in the attitude of sacrifice. And on earth, until the end of the age, on the altars of the Church, under the appearances of bread and wine, he goes on, in his extravagant love, giving out his Body, pouring out his Blood.

He who was once given, slain on the Cross, poured out, pierced, will never take back his gift, his gift of

89

himself. He will never gather into himself his Eucharistic fragmentation in order to be one with himself. Even as the risen Lord he lives as the One who has given himself and has poured himself out.[27]

This was a favourite theme of St Teresa of Avila:

The Father gave us his Son once and for all to die for us, and thus he is our own; yet he does not want the gift to be taken from us until the end of the world but would have it left to be a help to us every day.[28]

The Resurrection and Ascension, the going to the Father, are not a withdrawal of the Son-Gift. On the contrary, as the Farewell Discourse makes clear, they make possible, through the sending of the Spirit, a new intimacy and mode of presence (cf. John 16:16ff.).

Jesus' Eucharistic gesture of self-distribution to his Apostles, and through them to the world, is a definitive, eschatological and thus irreversible gesture. The Father's Word made flesh is definitively given and distributed by him and is never to be taken back. Neither the Resurrection from the dead nor the "Ascension" as "going to the Father" (Jn 16:18) are a countermovement to Incarnation, Passion and Eucharist.[29]

Jesus bears the marks of his Passion in his risen Body. "The Crucified, and he alone, is the Risen One".[30] He stands for ever, in his crucified and risen humanity, as "the slain Lamb" (Rev. 5:6).

This implies much more than that he merely stands before the Father as mediator in virtue of his acquired merits; likewise more than that he merely continues in an unbloody manner the "self-giving" he accomplished in a bloody manner on earth. It ultimately means that the Father's act of self-giving by which, throughout all created space and time, he pours out the Son is the definitive revealing of the Trinitarian act itself in which the "Persons" are God's "relations", forms of absolute self-giving and loving fluidity. In the Eucharist the Creator has succeeded in making the finite creaturely structure so fluid – without fragmenting or violating it ("No one takes my life from me", Jn 10:18) – that it is able to become the bearer of the Triune life.[31]

By placing the Eucharist in the context of the Lord's Incarnation and bodily Resurrection, Balthasar helps us understand the impossibility of the view that the Eucharist is a "bare commemoration", a sacrifice of merely vocal praise and thanksgiving. To say Eucharist is to say Sacrifice. For Christian thanksgiving is not a verbal invocation but the *Verbum incarnatum*. The *sacrificium laudis* is a slaughtered Lamb. The supreme thanksgiving to God the Father was given by the incarnate Son when he gave his All, his body as well as his soul, to the Father on Calvary. There can be no "spiritual" thanksgiving without communion in Christ's Sacrifice in the flesh. We receive the grace to offer "ourselves, our souls and bodies" by first offering and then eating the Paschal Lamb. Adrienne saw this very clearly. St Paul speaks of Christians "sharing the sufferings of Christ" (cf. Phil. 3:10), by which he means that Christians, by the grace of their Head, are able to offer their sufferings, in union with his, to the Father, thereby doing something beautiful for the Church (cf. Col. 1:24). Adrienne realized that this bearing of burdens in the Communion of Saints is only possible because daily, on the altar, the Lord places his sacrificed Body and Blood in the hands of his Bride to draw her more deeply into his Cross and so into the power of the Resurrection.

The Eucharistic Body enables the Church to partici-

pate in the Cross . . . For me to be able to suffer for
the Lord he must already live in me. If I do not
accept his Sacrifice, if I do not receive his Communion, then I stand outside and cannot suffer for
him.[32]

Where the Eucharist is regarded as a merely com-
memorative meal, Christ's saving Passion remains
locked away in history, accessible only by mental
recall. The Catholic doctrine is, by contrast, that, on
the altar, the Lord's saving work is "revived in the
midst of the years" (Hab. 3:2), earthed in the here and
now. Unbloodily, sacramentally, Christ's Sacrifice is
daily re-presented and offered for the living and the
dead, applied to Everyman's need and weakness, so
that our actual life's journey may be – through, with
and in the Son – a passage to the Father. Georges
Bernanos, that great Christian novelist, of whom
Balthasar wrote a long and detailed study, put down
these words in his diary a short time before his death
in 1948.

Just as he sacrifices himself on each altar where
Mass is offered, so he begins to die again in each
man at the moment of his agony. We will all that he
wills, but we do not know that we will it. Sin makes
us live on the surface of our lives; we only enter in
ourselves to die, and there it is he awaits us.[33]

One of Balthasar's favourite words is *Hingabe*, a richly
suggestive term, connoting surrender, devotion, sacrifice, giving up, giving away. It is the fundamental act
of the Son, as God and as man. Everything in Christianity is for giving away; keeping means certain loss
(cf. Luke 9:24). This is how God lives as Trinity. This is
how the Son made man lived and died on earth and
lives on for ever in the Eucharist. And this is how,
through his given-out Body and poured-out Blood, we
are to live in the Church, in the Communion of Saints.

7
LADY DAY, GOOD FRIDAY, ALL SAINTS' DAY

The mysteries of March bear fruit, through the Mass, in a mystery celebrated each November – the Communion of Saints. Through our Eucharistic communion in the sacrificed flesh and blood of the Son we enter into communion with the Father in the Holy Spirit and thus with one another, a fellowship that bridges time and space and death. Because of the Son's Death and Resurrection "for us", we are enabled as his members to live and suffer and die "for one another", and thereby we reveal that God himself is a communion of Three Persons who exist for each other in one divine substance. Christian existence is "pro-existence".

> The insertion of the faithful into the body and thus the work of Christ has the necessary consequence that they share . . . in his "for us".[1]

Baptismal incorporation into Christ has dramatic consequences for every Christian, even though they may not be apparent on the stage of world history.

> It means an extension of the individual's sphere of action, which is unimaginable in the order of creation. The individual Christian is no longer an isolated individual, but, in St Paul's imagery, someone who has been incorporated into the organism and blood-circulation of the Mystical Body.[2]

In Christ, says Balthasar, human beings become Catholic, personal yet deprivatized, sharing, in some way, in the Lord's own "concrete universality". This communication to men of Christ's own catholicity is what we mean by the *communio sanctorum*.[3] St Paul makes the point more simply when he speaks of the Church as Christ's Body. We are members, limbs, not only of Christ but of one another (cf. Eph. 4:25; 1 Cor. 12:26). In and through the Head who bore the load of the whole world's sin on the Cross, the members are enabled to bear one another's burdens (cf. Gal. 6:2). When one limb is happy, the others share his joy; when one suffers, the others feel his pain (cf. 1 Cor. 12:26).

Everything in the Mystical Body is for giving away. The spiritual goods which each member possesses are not for himself alone but for the whole Body. Every good work is Catholic, of an incalculable fruitfulness. Any comfort I receive, says St Paul, through Christ from the Father, is for you; anything I suffer I offer up in union with Christ for your salvation (cf. 2 Cor. 1:3ff.). Such influence of one member for the good of another, such "reversibility of merits", is unlimited. It spans time and space and death. It links every continent. It unites earth and Purgatory and Heaven. The French writer Léon Bloy, the friend of Jacques and Raïssa Maritain, captured the idea in these noble words:

> An act of love, the stirring of genuine compassion, sings the praises of God from Adam to the end of the world, heals the sick, comforts the desperate, stills storms, frees prisoners, converts unbelievers, shields the whole human race.[4]

Adrienne and the Communion of Saints

Adrienne was received into the Church by Balthasar on All Saints' Day 1940. The feast was providentially appropriate, for Adrienne's mission, with which Balthasar cooperated so closely, was to revive in the Church a deep sense of living and praying in the Communion of Saints. It was for this that Adrienne was given a host of mystical graces, enabling her to enjoy an extraordinary intimacy with the inhabitants of Heaven, especially Our Lady and St Ignatius Loyola. During Mass she would see the church filled with concelebrating angels and saints. With the Mother of God she had an almost homely, woman-to-woman kind of friendship.[5] The saints showed her the way they prayed, their weaknesses as well as their strengths, revealing heaven as a truly human place, open to earth. The first volume of *Das Allerheiligenbuch* is a wonderful book. It not only shows us how the saints pray but "invites us – by contagion, as it were – to pray ourselves".[6]

The *communio sanctorum* is the Church as commonwealth, the Mystical Body as "treasury", a "continually overflowing richness on which all the poor may draw".[7] Catholic theology has long spoken of the treasury of the merits of Christ, Our Lady, and the saints (this is part of the doctrine of indulgences). Adrienne adds to this the idea of a "treasury of prayer".

It makes no difference whether at any particular moment hundreds of thousands are praying, or a few, or perhaps no one. The dialogue is never broken off, and the relation of love between the Bride and the heavenly Bridegroom is always fresh and flowing. What the Church receives as grace, as prayer, as dialogue, is put at the disposal of all who pray as a support to their prayer.[8]

We never pray alone. We pray always with our fellow members in the Mystical Body, in living communion with the angels and saints. Our little prayer is always joined to the great and unceasing prayer of the whole Bride to the Bridegroom and so to his dialogue of love with the Father in the Holy Spirit.

Adrienne speaks of how, through Christ, in the Spirit, we can allow the angels and saints to "take over" our prayer. When we are tired, when we are ill, we can let ourselves be carried on the tide of adoration and intercession that flows from the blessed.

There is a perpetual prayer of the Church, of the individual in her, to God, which rings out like a kind of heavenly music. It is always heard and received in Heaven. Sometimes you are too tired to pray. All you can do is just think somehow of God and rejoice in him, or like a sick child just gaze at Mother or watch for a moment the business of the angels. It can then happen suddenly that you hear this kind of prayer-music and are seized by it . . . You are seized by the fact that here and now, at this very moment, so many people are really praying, that so many too are praying in joy, quite simply, and, faced with the radiance of God, have forgotten their own destiny, their personal sorrow, their responsibilities; they have become unimportant to themselves . . . You make up your mind to pray and you do, and suddenly you are no longer alone but singing in harmony with the universal melody of prayer.[9]

The *communio sanctorum*, for Adrienne, did not just mean fellowship with the saints in Heaven and the holy souls in Purgatory. It meant, too, a special kind of sharing with her brethren on earth. In 1938 Balthasar's mentor, Henri (now Cardinal) de Lubac, published his classic study of the "social aspects" of

Catholicism.[10] Balthasar passed on its essential message to Adrienne when preparing her for reception into the Church. The seed fell on fertile and receptive ground.

When I was instructing her, I strongly emphasized that the distinctive mark of Catholicism was solidarity: Christ's vicarious work for all and of his members for one another. Now she received a direct experience of this solidarity. On this first occasion it was the experience of guilt . . . By becoming more and more aware of her own guiltiness and weakness, she experienced at the same time the mysteriously social character of all human guilt . . . She felt solidarity with every sin committed. Later she would ask me whether, *per impossibile*, someone who had not committed any sins could still confess. To begin with, I said No. Then she explained further: in a certain sense she shared in every murder and adultery that happened anywhere in the world. She knew precisely that a connection existed. If she were different, so would these unknown people be. And, as far as she herself was concerned, she was capable of any sin; it was only a wonder of God's grace that she had been preserved from it.[11]

This interesting passage shows an individualistic Calvinist feeling of guilt being transfigured into a Catholic sense of solidarity. It is a Yes of ardent charity to a vocation of intercession and vicarious reparation. Adrienne wanted to relieve her brethren of their burdens. When she was a little girl, on a visit to a children's ward with her eye-doctor father, she asked if she could be blind for a little while so that a blind boy could see.[12] In later life, in the Church, by intercession and the practice of penance, Adrienne tried to take something of other people's guilt and pain from them. She did not do this, of course, by her own resources but simply and humbly by the grace of the sin-bearing Lamb of God. During the war, though physically resident in neutral Switzerland, Adrienne plunged deep into the agonies of her fellow men and women.

> We sat on the terrace above the Rhine. On the far bank is Germany. She feels the suffering, the world's anguish. At that very time the great Russian offensive begins. A million dead, the Russians say. She groans aloud. She hears clearly, in her own ears, the cries of death, the screaming of mothers, those who weep and give up their sons, and the even worse screams of those who do not give up their sons, who do not want to weep. In the river's roar and the faint hum of the city she hears the noise of the world. It seems peaceful, but in reality it is very different. In reality everything is screaming, every person, every creature. I hear the cries quite clearly. I can hardly bear it. Everywhere – deep down – is fear.[13]

Throughout her life, Adrienne suffered terribly: in spirit with inner darkness and Godforsakenness, in body with diabetes, heart trouble, near blindness, and finally a lingering mortal illness. She offered it all up in union with Christ to the Father to ease in some way the load oppressing her fellow men.

> As soon as a person has inwardly said Yes to some trial, to suffering, it is used further afield and has an effect on other people. Even without explicit offering up . . . or special prayer.[14]

Suffering in itself is not good, and the good God does not want it for his creatures, but, in his providence and by the grace of his crucified Son, it can be for the good when lovingly offered up – in expiation for our sins, for the salvation of our brethren, and to God's greater glory. Nothing is in vain. The one thing needful is humble assent, a child-like, Mary-like Yes.

"Horizontal" and "Vertical" Communion

The wonderful communion of the members of the Mystical Body among themselves is entirely dependent on their communion, through Christ, with the Trinity. St John suggests this in his first letter, where *koinônia* with the "Us" of the Church is linked with *koinônia* with the Father and the Son (cf. 1 John 1:3).[15] Whatever the members do for each other "horizontally" is made possible by the grace that flows "vertically" from the Father, by the working of the Holy Spirit, through the crucified and risen manhood of the Son.

> The foundation of the "Communion of Saints" has to be goodness "in person", the goodness that forges unity.[16]

As Origen saw, the inter-knitting of the faithful derives from their communion, by grace, with the Trinity.[17] Again, Augustine says that the Holy Spirit who is the unity of Father and Son is also what binds together the *communio sanctorum*.[18] This is reflected in the third section of the Apostles' Creed, where the Communion of Saints is appropriated to the Holy Spirit.

Only through the power of the Head, only in the Spirit who is the "soul" of his Mystical Body, can the members have a salvific effect on each other. If we are to understand the "co-redemptive" vocation of the Church, "the distance between 'Head' and 'members' must be maintained in all circumstances".[19] As St Thomas taught and then later Cajetan and the Council of Trent, it is not strictly we who merit or offer satisfaction but Christ who merits and offers satisfaction in us.[20] The image of the vine brings this out clearly. The vine needs the branches as organs if it is to bear fruit, yet the branches are utterly dependent on the vine ("without me you can do nothing", John 15:5). Its circulating juices are the only source of fruitfulness. And so the contribution of the branches is letting those juices flow freely.

> The activity [of the branches] consists in letting what the vine does happen, in assenting to what it has fashioned and made possible beyond their own capacities. The fruitfulness of the branches is inseparably two things: their very own, yet totally bestowed, an utter gift.[21]

Because of the dependence of the Church's "horizontal" communion on her "vertical" communion, through Christ, with the Trinity, we can see why the historical ambiguity of the phrase *communio sanctorum* has a positive value. Does it mean the fellowship of holy persons (the *sancti*) or the sharing of holy things (the *sancta* of the Eucharist)? The point is that both meanings are necessary for the full doctrine. Only by the holy gifts can we be a holy community. It is through our sacramental participation in Christ's "pro-existent" Sacrifice that we come to exist for one another. St Thomas explains it clearly in his exposition of the Apostles' Creed. The good of Christ the Head, the saving power and grace of his Passion, is communicated to his members through the sacraments. Then, in and through that power, the good of one member is communicated to another.[22]

Among twentieth-century Catholic writers, no one has gone more deeply into the mystery of the Communion of Saints than Georges Bernanos. In his screenplay *The Carmelites*, based on the novel by

Gertrud von Le Fort, later scored as an opera by
Poulenc, he tells the story of the Carmelites of Com-
piègne martyred during the French Revolution.[23] As
the clouds of death gather (Bernanos wrote it when he
himself was dying), many of the nuns are bravely
ready, but Sister Blanche of the Agony of Christ
cannot master her fear of death. Her sisters – out of
love, by prayer – take that fear from her and upon
themselves. The old Prioress dies a strange and dis-
turbing death, one that does not seem to fit her. The
Sub-Prioress, Marie de l'Incarnation, urges the community to take an oath of martyrdom, and yet she
does not die with the others; her cross is to go on
living. As for Blanche herself, in the end she dies for
Christ without dread. This "substitution and
exchange" is not achieved by the sisters' unaided
resources, but only through, with, and in Christ, in
whose "adorable Heart" in Gethsemane all human
anguish was divinized. There is no hybris in the
martyrs. However poor they may be, they know that
their Lord and Master was infinitely poorer. They
imitate him humbly, at a distance.[24] It is by grace – by
the grace of the mysteries of March – that the *communio sanctorum* is a living and dramatic reality. In the
dying words of another Bernanos character, "all is
grace".[25]

Three

The Incarnation, the Descent into Hell and the Resurrection

8
LADY DAY AND HOLY SATURDAY

The mysteries of March are mysteries of descent. In March the Son of God descended into the Virgin's womb, into human life; and in March, too, he descended into human death, into the womb of Hell. St Ephrem praises both movements:

The Shepherd of all flew down
in search of Adam, the sheep that had strayed;
on his shoulders he carried him, taking him up:
he was an offering for the Lord of the flock,
Blessed is his descent!

He sprinkled dew and life-giving rain
on Mary, the thirsty earth.
Like a seed of wheat he fell again to Sheol,
to spring up as a whole sheaf, as the new Bread.
Blessed is his offering.[1]

Balthasar, like the Church Fathers, sees the whole saving economy of the Son, from the Virgin's undefiled womb to Joseph's unused tomb, as a coming down: "for us men and our salvation he came down from Heaven". The Incarnation is the self-abasement of true God not the promotion of a mere man.[2] Forty days after his glorious Resurrection, Christ ascends, in the fullness of his humanity, to the Father, but he does so as the One who first descended, to assume our humanity, in the Virgin's womb. As Jesus says in

St John's gospel, "No one has ascended into Heaven but he who descended from heaven, the Son of Man" (John 3:13).

Now, for Balthasar, as for the Fathers, the language of descent, when applied to the Incarnation, does not imply local movement or indeed any kind of alteration of the Logos. As St Leo says in his *Tome*, "the Son of God, descending from his heavenly throne, yet not leaving the glory of the Father, enters into this lowly world".[3] The descent is the assumption of what is below, not the desertion of what is above.[4] "Above" and "below" are irreducible and universal metaphors, independent of any pre-scientific, "three-tier" model of the universe.[5] Balthasar points out that the imagery of descent and ascent belongs to the universal symbolism of natural man. Sunlight, and with it life, shines down on man's face from above; the grave's darkness is below his feet.[6] This explains the aptness of the analogy of falling: fallen man has collapsed into death, physical and spiritual, lies prostrate, weak and wounded in the dust of the Jericho road. Only if the divine Samaritan bends down to him from above can he be saved.[7]

The great value of the language of descent is that it forcefully describes the divine initiative in redemption, the prevenient love and mercy of the Father, who loved us first and sent his Son for the expiation of our sins (cf. 1 John 4:19). He does not wait for us to pick ourselves up, for we are powerless to do so. He makes the first move. This is the message, says St Irenaeus, of the Virginal Conception.

> The Lord himself, who is Emmanuel from the Virgin, is the sign of our salvation, since it was the Lord himself who saved them, for they did not have the wherewithal to be saved.[8]

Balthasar believes that the descendant movement of

revelation is a sign of Christianity's utter uniqueness among the world's religions. Those of the Far East, for example, picture man as trying to "construct a relationship with God",[9] flying up to the divine on the wings of philosophy or meditation. On this flight, the human body is inevitably seen as an encumbrance to be left below and behind. The same ascendant, spirit-ualizing impulse can be detected in Neo-Platonism and, much later, in German Idealism, with its "Prom-ethean" tendency to romanticize the upward, self-transcendent surge of created spirit. The first volume of Balthasar's first book, *Die Apokalypse der deutschen Seele*, published in 1937 and later reprinted with the title *Prometheus*, documents the evolution of this theme in German Idealism.[10] Philosophical Pro-metheanism is, of its nature, anti-incarnational. Like the mythological figure of Prometheus the rebel, it wants man to assert himself and rise up; it does not want God to come down. The fire of fulfilment is to be snatched not received. Here is the starting-point for all those ideologies, whether of the right or the left, which reject God and the Incarnation of God, and instead absolutize man and his capacity for self-fulfilment.[11]

Descendit de caelis, descendit ad infernos. In order to seek and to save the lost, God the Son, without leaving his Father's side, comes down from Heaven. And then, being found in human form, he humbles himself and goes deeper and deeper into the abyss of our wretchedness until he reaches its lowest level – Sheol, the place of the dead. The Byzantine Liturgy, on Great and Holy Saturday, senses that the dark descent of that day is only the final stage of a long downward journey that began, thirty-three years earlier, in the pure womb of Mary: "To earth hast Thou come down, O Master, to save Adam: and not finding him on earth, Thou has descended into Hell,

107

seeking him there."[12]

With Balthasar's help, I want to look at the awful mystery of the Descent into Hell and to consider its relationship to the first of the descendant March mysteries, the Incarnation. Wilhelm Maas has described Balthasar as *"the* theologian of the Descent into Hell".[13] The attention which he gave to this article of the creed was due, as he himself admitted on many occasions, to his relationship with Adrienne von Speyr, who each Holy Week, from 1941 until 1965, was given the grace to share spiritually in the sufferings of Christ. This sharing reached its climax in a mystical Descent into Hell, which began shortly after 3 pm on Good Friday and lasted until the early hours of Easter Sunday. From *The Heart of the World* (written in 1943) to the final volumes of his theological trilogy, many direct echoes of Adrienne's Paschal Triduum experiences are to be found in Balthasar's writings.[14] He does not, of course, imagine for one moment that what was disclosed to Adrienne adds to or subtracts from the deposit of revelation. His claim is simply that, through her, for the good of the whole Church, the Holy Spirit has thrown a fresh light on a hitherto little considered article of the faith. Her theology incorporates all the insights of the tradition, and yet it is more than just a repetition of propositions from the past.

> In addition to all the traditional elements, one cannot fail to recognize the newness of her central assertions. These and these alone make possible a synthesis of what hitherto had been fragments into a living, highly fruitful whole.[15]

Holy Saturday, the day of the Descent, lies midway between the Cross of Good Friday and the Resurrection of Easter Sunday and so constitutes "the central point of all revelation and theology", the "necessary" conclusion of the Cross and the "necessary" presupposition of the resurrection.[16] As Adrienne says, "the Lord does not rise from the Cross, but from the Hell of Holy Saturday".[17] The Resurrection of Christ is after all, as the Roman Canon says, a resurrection *ab inferis*, from the underworld.

The Descent into Hell in Tradition and Scripture

The Descent into Hell made its first credal appearance in the East in the second half of the fourth century and eventually found its way into what is now the received text of the Apostles' Creed. It has occasionally surfaced in the teaching of councils, both local and ecumenical. For example, the Fourth General Council of the Lateran (1215) includes it in its Definition against the Albigensians and Cathars:

> He descended into Hell, rose again from the dead, and ascended into heaven. But he descended in soul, rose again in the flesh, and ascended equally in both.[18]

The council here recapitulates the teaching of the Fathers, particularly those who had written against Apollinarianism, the heresy which denied that the Word assumed a rational soul.[19] It is truly the person of the Son of God who descends into Hell, but he descends not in his divinity but in the human soul hypostatically united to him, while his human body, likewise united, lies in the still of the tomb. This defines what the Descent is; it says nothing of what it achieves.

All the major traditions of the New Testament agree that Jesus is raised *ek nekrôn*, "from among those who are dead", and thus, by implication, from the "place

109

of the dead". In line with this, the passage in St Matthew's Passion narrative referring to the "bodies of the saints" being raised up and "coming out of the tombs after [Jesus'] Resurrection" (cf. Matt. 27:51b–53) is applied to the Descent into Hell as early as St Ignatius of Antioch: the anticipated resurrection of the bodies of the just is the direct effect of Christ's visit to their souls in Sheol.[20] Similarly, the "heart of the earth" in which the Son prophesies he will rest, Jonah-like, for three days (cf. Matt. 12:40) is almost certainly the underworld of the dead.[21]

The Descent into Hell seems to be connected in some special way with the preaching of St Peter. First, in the Acts of the Apostles, in his speech on the day of Pentecost, Peter cites Ps. 15:10 as a prophecy of the Resurrection: David foresaw that Christ's soul would not be abandoned to Hades, nor his flesh see corruption (cf. Acts 2:31). Then there are two texts in 1 Peter which refer to Our Lord preaching to the dead (cf. 1 Peter 3:18–21a; 4:6). The distinguished protestant exegete, Charles Cranfield, has defended the traditional interpretation of these two passages. Moreover, he argues that it would be unwise to dismiss the doctrine of the Descent as an intrusion from pagan mythology.[22]

The implication of these last two Petrine texts would seem to be that, between Good Friday afternoon and his Resurrection in the early hours of Easter Sunday morning, the soul of Jesus is in "the place of the dead", the "underworld", what the Old Testament calls *Sheol* and the New Testament *Hades*. In the earliest parts of the Old Testament, Sheol is the neutral abode of the dead, the destination of all mortal men, whether good or bad. With the development of belief in an eschatological resurrection of the dead, Sheol becomes an "intermediate state", with different compartments for the godly and ungodly. This pre-resurrection separation is an anticipation of their final destinies after the general resurrection and last judgement ("Paradise" for the virtuous, "Gehenna" for the wicked). At both stages in the development of Israel's faith, Sheol is a place of abandonment and isolation, of darkness (Job 10:21f.), of silence (Ps. 93:17), from which no one returns (Job 7:9; 10:21), in which there is no joy (Ecclesiasticus 14:11–17), no knowledge of what happens on earth (Job 14:21ff.), no praise of God (Ps. 113:17; Is. 38:18).[23]

The Hades of the New Testament, like Sheol, appears to be a temporary state; in the Apocalypse, St John speaks of it being destroyed, thrown into the lake of fire (Rev. 20:14). In fact, it is the Old Testament Sheol with a new, Greek name: the intermediate state of good and bad (in their different compartments) prior to the general resurrection at the end of history. In the story of Dives and Lazarus, it is presented by Our Lord as the state or place of the ungodly awaiting resurrection. Gehenna, by contrast, is the post-resurrection place of eternal punishment, where the wicked are tormented in body and soul (cf. Matt. 5:22).

Balthasar argues that Sheol-Hades is not just, as the Biblical theology textbooks say, an undeveloped Hebrew *idea* of the after-life. Before the Cross and Resurrection of the incarnate Word, Sheol really was the only after-life the souls of the dead could enjoy. As St Thomas shows, before Christ, though the good angels beheld the face of the Father, no human souls enjoyed the Beatific Vision.[24] Balthasar takes the argument a stage further: not only the "human" Heaven, but Hell and Purgatory, too, are the direct effect of Christ's Descent into Sheol.

Balthasar and Adrienne rescue the Descent into Hell from, on the one hand, dilution or embarrassed silence and, on the other, from distortion and melo-

111

dramatic exaggeration. The Byzantine tradition, in its liturgy and iconography, has retained a strong sense of the Descent, but it tends, in Balthasar's opinion, to interpret the mystery in too narrowly triumphal terms. Luther goes to the other extreme and claims that Christ was vicariously damned, a damnation which is first realized in the dereliction of the Cross. Balthasar rejects this interpretation: Jesus is a totally holy Yes to the Father and so cannot make the irrevocable No of the damned his own. The hallmark of the Adrienne-Balthasar theology of the Descent, what distinguishes it from other interpretations, is its Trinitarian perspective.

> Hell is a Trinitarian event . . . on Holy Saturday the Son (as man and Redeemer) is introduced to the dark mystery of the Father, something which can only happen in mystery and in silence.[25]

The Descent into Hell and the Incarnation

According to Adrienne, the Descent into Hell "is the ultimate consequence of the Incarnation".[26] The Son of God, in order to redeem us, assumes human nature and in that nature makes his own every stage and state of human existence. And so he dies a truly human death, his soul being separated from his body, though neither is separated from the divine hypostasis of the Word.[27] During the three days of death it is truly the body of God the Son that lies in the tomb and truly his soul that descends into Hell. Our compassionate High Priest wants to know at first hand our every experience, not only our dying but our being dead. And so he descends into Hell to share the state of those who are dead.

Adrienne's intuition is in harmony with Patristic

preaching and Scholastic reflection. For example, in his homily on Holy Saturday, St John Damascene calls the Descent into Hell "the culmination of the divine economy . . . the garland on the incarnation of God the Word".[28] St Thomas, similarly, argues that Our Lord goes down to the dead not because of any insufficiency in the suffering endured on the Cross, but because of the logic of the Incarnation: he wants to share all the disabilities of sinful men (other than those, of course, which imply a defect of grace). And so his body lies in the tomb, his soul descends into Hell, so that "in both ways he might be like his brethren".[29] He suffers the whole penalty of sin in order to expiate the whole of sin. The purpose of the Incarnation was to "seek and to save the lost", weakened and wounded Adam. Hell is where the search finally ended. The homily attributed to St Epiphanius, now read in the Divine Office on Holy Saturday, expresses this beautifully.[30]

Jesus does not descend into Hell as Risen but as Dead. As St Thomas says, between dying on Good Friday and being raised from the dead on Easter Sunday, Our Lord is not a man but a *dead man*.[31] And the obedience which, according to Balthasar, takes him into the underworld is likewise the obedience of "the dead Christ".[32] Unlike the mythological heroes, Orpheus and Odysseus, who went into Hell alive, as did Dante, Christ's Descent follows real human death, the separation of soul from body. In his soul the Son of God experiences the passivity, the powerlessness, of every separated human spirit in Sheol.

Christ did not (as in the icons of the Eastern Church) descend as the victorious Risen One – Holy Saturday is not Easter – but as the Dead One, who no longer speaks as the Word of God, or rather "has become the silent Word of the Father". And so we have to learn to share this silence between Death and Resurrection.[33]

The divine Word enters the total speechlessness of death. He becomes "the Father's silent Word". And yet this silence is the Father's most eloquent announcement of his love for us. Once again, we see the interconnection of the mysteries of March: the descent into the wordlessness of infant human life in the womb makes possible and foreshadows the descent into the wordlessness of death in Sheol. In fact, Balthasar says, there is something childlike about the whole manner in which Jesus suffers and dies.[34]

God the Son, in his human soul, descends into Hell so he can share mankind's final infirmity – not only dying but deadness. He enters into solidarity with the dead.

> The ultimate consequence of the redemptive mission he has received from the Father is to be in solidarity with the dead, or rather to be in solidarity with that death which for the first time makes the dead really dead.[35]

Paradoxically, the place of the dead, Sheol, the only destiny for the just who died before Christ, is the very opposite of solidarity. As depicted by the Old Testament, it means helpless isolation, inactivity, remoteness from men and from God.[36] Christ's very presence in this world of solitude is transforming and salvific: in conjunction with his Resurrection and Ascension, it makes possible an after-life of transcendent and indestructible solidarity, the communion of his members in Heaven, in Purgatory, and on earth.

114

The Descent and the Trinity

Balthasar sees Christ's "exploration" of Hell as "an (economic) Trinitarian event".[37] What does he mean by this extraordinary assertion?

First, the Descent is a filial act, the experience (in his human soul) of the only-begotten Son, the Second Person of the Blessed Trinity. It is, in fact, the final consequence of that human obedience of his which, as we have seen, expresses his divine and eternal love of the Father in the Spirit. Here we see an obedience to the Father that reaches beyond life into the ultimate passivity of being dead.[38] It is the literal instance of what St Francis of Assisi once called "corpse obedience".[39] The ever-greatness of the Son's eternal love is expressed, in human deadness, in the form of "super-obedience" (*Übergehorsam*), the Father's final "excessive demand" (*Überforderung*).[40] Here is a humble compliance that vanquishes rebellious Satan: his cunning is overcome by the "super-cunning" of love,[41] and he himself is pushed into the "hindmost chamber of Hell".[42] What the First Adam wrecked by his No, the Second has renewed by his Yes. Balthasar's theology is in harmony with the great Byzantine sermons for Holy Saturday. For example, in one by St Germanus of Constantinople, the soul of Jesus says to Adam's shade: "I have come not to curse you for your disobedience but to bless you with my obedience".[43]

The Son goes through Hell in order to return to the Father

The Descent into Hell is the final stage of the Son's Paschal journey to his Father.[44] Before his rising again and ascending to the Heaven of the Father, he descends into the Hell of Adam. This downward journey is not a detour but "the shortest way to the Father".[45] How can this be? First, because, according to Balthasar, Hell belongs to God the Father, by a special appropriation, inasmuch as he is the creator of our freedom, and Hell is perverted freedom's last frontier.[46] So much does the Son love the Father that he is prepared to look for him in the *limbus*, the "lumber-room", of his creation where, at least to all appearances, he is not and cannot be.[47]

Hell is the Father's "reservation" as Creator. In creating the world, he foresaw and permitted the terrible possibility of man misusing his freedom to the point of irrevocably rejecting love. Linked thus with the making of a world of finite freedom, Hell is "a kind of mirrored reflection of the chaos at the beginning of creation", the world's "second chaos".[48] In the beginning, the Father, through his Word and his Spirit of love, created the world out of the "chaos" of non-being. On Holy Saturday, the Word "as a dead man", to fulfil his mission of recreation, enters into Hell, "the world's 'second chaos'", not the "neutral" void of non-being, but the pit of darkness to which Adam consigned himself and all his sons and daughters.[49] Once more, we must remember that we are still talking about Sheol, the common destiny of all departed human spirits before the coming of Christ. Hell, even as the *limbus Patrum*, is a place of unhappiness and abandonment.

In Hell the Son confronts that dark mystery which is the Father's permission of sin. This non-prevention of moral evil has two sides: God's infinite respect for his rational creatures' freedom; and his loving determination to save men from the consequences of their self-destructive folly.

The Son sinks straight into the supreme mystery of the Father, the creator of the world: the power given

116

to the devil to seduce the human race. This mystery of the Father is buried in this darkness. God is powerful enough to make his light shine everywhere, powerful enough to prevent evil establishing itself or just to suppress it. The fact that he did not is what is most impenetrable about him. But men had to be free. They were not created perfect, they had to grow in order to come close to God. God wanted to give his heaven only to adult sons. This space of freedom contains the divine darkness and the means of sinning. But the darkness of God too is a mystery of love.[50]

In everything the Son does as man, there is a twofold reference – to the Father and to mankind. By obeying the Father unto death, he loves mankind "to the end". He is abandoned by the Father precisely so that mankind's sin which he bears can be wholly borne away. And in Hell, in his spiritual soul, he descends into a double darkness: that defect of light which is sin, and that dazzling excess of light which is the bosom of the Father.[51] The Descent into Hell is, after all, part of his mission, which, as we have seen, for Balthasar as for St Thomas, manifests and prolongs his eternal procession from the Father by way of generation. The sending into Hell is, therefore, the dramatic expression, in human mortality, of his divine origin.

The Son's going through Hell as a mystery of the Father is an indication of the Father's fatherhood with respect to the Son. Through the darkness of Hell the Son feels his way into the mystery of origin.[52]

In the eternal, inner life of the Godhead the Son loves the Father in the Holy Spirit. In his manhood, with his human will, the Son expresses that filial love in the form of obedience. This, too, as we have seen, is

117

carried out "in the Spirit". What role, then, does the Holy Spirit play in the final act of Christ's obedience, his Descent into Hell? We have already seen how, on the Cross, paradoxically, the Spirit was revealed as the bond of communion between Father and Son at the very moment of the Son's abandonment by the Father. The paradox continues in Sheol.

The Father answers the Son's Spirit-filled human act of self-surrender by showing him Hell. Why? Because the Father loves mankind and wants his Son to share, for the sake of redemption, the furthest reaches of human experience. This does not mean that he loves the world more than he loves his Son. That is impossible. In any case, as St Thomas says, it is by the very same Spirit of love that the Father loves the Son and us.[53] And so, astonishingly, the Descent serves the revelation of the Trinity.

> In Hell the highest distinction of the persons and their ineffable unity are disclosed. Where the Son thought he was most abandoned by the Father, abandonment is used to burst open the prison of abandonment, and to admit the Son, together with the world redeemed, into the Heaven of the Father.[54]

What is the Hell into which Christ descends?

In the third part of the *Summa Theologiae*, St Thomas asks whether Christ descended into the "Hell of the Damned". His answer is that the soul of Christ had an effect on all the inhabitants of the nether regions – the damned to confute them in their unbelief and malice; those detained in Purgatory to give them the hope of attaining glory; and the holy fathers of the Old Testament, detained only because of Original Sin, to infuse into them the light of eternal glory. But in its essence, the soul of Christ visited only the last of these – the *limbus Patrum*.[55]

Balthasar does not disagree with St Thomas' answer: the soul of Christ did not descend into Hell in the sense of the place or state of eternal punishment. He did not himself, as the Reformers imagine, become "one of the damned". The soul of Christ is an unshakeable Yes to the Father; even his Descent into Hell is an act of obedience to God. It is unthinkable that the absolutely sinless Son of God could experience the torment that only one who irrevocably says No to God can know. Nonetheless, Balthasar regards the Thomist question as wrongly posed. Before the coming of Christ, there was neither Hell nor Purgatory, only the single Sheol of the Old Testament, in which the souls of the Patriarchs were detained. The Hell of damnation exists only as a consequence of the Paschal Mystery.

> It is a theological error to project back the New Testament (Christological) concept of Hell onto the Old Testament and ask questions of Holy Saturday which are unanswerable because wrongly put. Augustine expresses himself very clearly on the subject of this theological replacement of Hades by Hell. Hell in the New Testament is a function of the event of Christ . . . before Christ ("before" in the ontological rather than chronological sense) there can be neither Hell nor Purgatory . . . but only that Hades . . . from which Christ wanted to deliver us by his solidarity with the dead.[56]

Sheol, even if divided into two compartments for the good and the bad, is for all its inhabitants "the place where God is absent".

> . . . where there is no longer the light of faith, hope, love, of participation in God's life; Hell [= Sheol] is

what the judging God condemned and cast out of his creation; it is filled with all that is irreconcilable with God, from which he turns away for all eternity. It is filled with the reality of all the world's godlessness, with the sum of the world's sin; therefore with precisely all of that from which the Crucified has freed the world. In Hell he encounters his own work of salvation, not in Easter triumph, but in the uttermost night of obedience, truly the "obedience of a corpse".[57]

At the Resurrection, Sheol, the state in which the Patriarchs languished, is left behind, but Christ takes Hell with him, the Hell of the New Testament, which is "the expression of His power to dispose, as judge, of eternal salvation or eternal damnation".[58] Hell is a christological concept.[59] It can be defined as the torment of those who have rejected the God who in his love descended even into Godlessness for them. Balthasar maintains that, while such a fate is a terrible possibility, the Church has never taught that it is an actuality for anyone. Of certain people the Church declares officially that they are in Heaven and may be venerated by the faithful. But of no soul, not even that of Judas, does she declare that it is in Hell. Balthasar is not, as some of his critics have maintained, reviving Origenistic universalism. He is, however, arguing against the Augustinian view of a thickly populated Hell.[60]

The "Activity" of Christ in Hell

In Hell the soul of the Son sees the sin of the world which he bore on the Cross.

The Son must "inspect whatever in the realm of creation is imperfect, unformed, chaotic", so as to lead into his own possession as Redeemer . . . This vision of chaos by the God-Man has become for us the condition of our vision of the Godhead.[61]

What he sees is sin without sinners: "the sin of the world become anonymous", "the accumulated aggregate of sheer sin", "the total mass of sin".[62] He encounters "that reality of sin which the Cross has separated from man and humanity, the reality of sin in the sense of what has been eternally rejected by God and definitively cast out of the world".[63] In his Passion the incarnate Son detaches sin from sinners and places it on his own shoulders. After his death he unloads it in Hell, consigning it to everlasting oblivion. But before he does so, in his spiritual soul he looks at sin in all its hideousness.

Adrienne says that in Hell Christ encounters the "effigies" of sinners, not animate beings but inert replicas. These the Lord leaves behind him, buried and forgotten, so that, through his Resurrection, the whole person may come gloriously alive.

> [The effigies] are whatever in each sinner God has condemned and cast out. What he had to throw into Hell in order to save the living person and make him through Christ into a child of God. The effigies are not unreal, because the sinful person has given away some of his own reality to sin. So every redeemed sinner has a kind of reproduction of himself in Hell.[65]

This idea of Christ descending into Hell in order to see has firm roots in the tradition. St Irenaeus, for example, says that "he descended beneath the earth to see with his own eyes the unfinished part of his creation".[66] In the thirteenth century the Franciscan theologian Alexander of Hales likewise argues that our enjoyment of the Beatific Vision depends on

Christ's vision of Hell.[67] Had he not confronted sin in all its ugliness, we would not be able to see him, with the Father and the Holy Spirit, in their Triune beauty. The most striking precedent to Balthasar's thought is to be found in the work of the fifteenth-century Cardinal and philosopher, Nicholas of Cusa, who says that, since Christ's suffering was "the greatest conceivable", it went as far as hellish pain (*usque ad poenam infernalem*).[68] Nicholas is not saying that the Lord experienced damnation, but rather that, in the deepest reaches of Hell, he saw second death, a vision which is the most total form of pain.

The Descent into Hell is a work of substitution. By going down into the pit, the sinless Son puts himself in the sinner's lowest place.

> Not only does he go to meet the Father where he most certainly is not, he also goes through [Hell] as the One he is (the sinless Son of the Father) and at the same time as the One he is not, inasmuch as he is the bearer of all the sin of the world.[69]

St Thomas makes a similar point when discussing the fittingness of the Descent.

> Now by sin man had merited not only the death of the body, but also the Descent into Hell or "second death". So it was fitting that he descended into Hell to preserve us from having to go there ourselves.[70]

The tradition has always been convinced that Our Lord's suffering for us, in body and in soul, was the greatest conceivable, embracing yet going beyond all the world's agony. Similarly, no one has descended more deeply into the abyss than the soul of the Son did on Holy Saturday. This is what changes the situation of sinful mankind: however deeply any man may plunge into Hell, whether in this life or in the life to come, Christ has gone deeper. As St Gregory the

122

Great says, he is *inferno profundior*, "deeper than Hell".[71]

Perhaps the most disconcerting thesis in Balthasar's treatise on the Descent is that, since the Son enters into real solidarity with the dead, there can be no question of him engaging in active combat or preaching. He shares the passivity of human death, and so what he "does" on Holy Saturday is contemplative and objective, whereas the Passion is active and subjective.[72] In Sheol he is one of the *refa'im*, in solidarity with the powerless. I say that this is the most disconcerting of Balthasar's claims because it is at odds with the long tradition, theological as well as literary and icongraphic, which sees Christ descending as Victor, the Harrower of Hell, the One who alone is "free among the dead". (One thinks, for example, of the eleventh-century mosaics of San Marco in Venice). It conflicts, too, with Scripture's clearest testimony to the Descent: St Peter's assertion that the departed soul of Jesus "preaches". The traditional image and the Balthasarian theology can be reconciled, so it seems to me, when we recall that it is precisely as passively dead that Christ actively preaches. The Word sounds most resonantly, with the Good News of sin's overcoming, when he lies in the silence of death. He conquered on Calvary by offering even defeat to the Father. And in Hell he is victorious by obediently accepting the downfall that is deadness. This is the constant refrain of the Byzantine liturgy on Great and Holy Saturday.

Going down to death, O Life immortal, Thou hast slain Hell with the dazzling light of Thy divinity . . . Of Thine own will descending as one dead beneath the earth, O Jesus, Thou leadest up the fallen from earth to Heaven.[73]

The Effects of the Descent into Hell

Christ's plumbing of Hell has transformed a prison into a way. Balthasar cites Gregory the Great:

> Christ descended into the very depths of the sea when he entered the deepest hell in order to retrieve the souls of his chosen ones. Before the redemption, the depth of the sea was not a way but a prison . . . But God has made this abyss into a way.[74]

The Lord can "take a walk" (*deambulare*) through the deepest hell because he is not impeded by the bonds of sin; he alone is "free among the dead". What is more, says Gregory – and this is a precious truth – the Lord who descended into the abyss during the *triduum mortis* descends now, with his risen power and joy, into the "desperate hearts" of men on earth.

The way through death to Heaven which Christ opens in Sheol is Purgatory.[75] Like Hell, it is christo-logical. Its foundation is closely connected with the institution of the Sacrament of Penance. Both are gifts of the Conqueror of Hell, both presuppose the bearing of sin on Good Friday and its unloading and burial on Holy Saturday. Purgatory is a kind of total Con-fession.[76]

> The possibility of instituting both Confession and Purgatory is something the Lord receives from the Cross. He bears all our sin, experiences it in a way he had never known before. He now sees at first-hand how deeply rooted it is in us and how radical the measures he takes must be, measures which are, of course, measures of love, though inevitably rigorous. He redeems us, and yet not in such a way that we can stand by indifferently, but by letting us share in his love unto eternal life. The mixture of

124

love and punishment, of joy and shame, both in Confession and Purgatory, shows that the Cross did not kill joy in the Lord, that, when he returns from the Cross and the underworld, he remains in the joyful decision to return the world to the Father.[77]

Heaven, too, as humanity's final bliss, where the souls of men see God face to face, is a fruit of the Descent. Before Christ's Descent, the good angels enjoyed the Beatific Vision, but no created human spirit did, not even the greatest sons of the Old Testament. That is why St John the Baptist is Christ's forerunner in Sheol as well as on earth.

Heaven, Purgatory, and Hell are all christological and therefore theological in character. As St Augustine says, "God himself is our place after this life".[78]

God is the "last thing" of the creature. Gained, he is Heaven; lost, he is Hell; examining, he is judgement; purifying, he is Purgatory. To him finite being dies, and through, to, and in him it rises. But this is God as he presents himself to the world, that is, in his Son, Jesus Christ, who is the revelation of God and therefore the whole essence of the last things.[79]

The Trinitarian God is a consuming fire, a living flame of love. When a Christian has died as the martyrs die, fully surrendering himself through Christ in the Spirit to the Father, the flame is heavenly bliss; when his surrender is real but incomplete, the flame burns to heal and purify; when the surrender is definitively rejected, when self is loved to the final contempt of God, the same fire is eternal torment.

The Ecclesiological Dimension: Sharing in the Descent

Our Lord shares his All with us. All that the Head does or has in his human nature is for sharing, by grace, with his members: his divine Father to be ours by baptismal adoption, his Spirit to fill our hearts; his Mother as our Mother too, his members and brethren to be ours in one communion; him as Victim to offer, him as food to eat; his Priesthood for appropriation in common or ministerial form. Since Head and Body are like one mystical person, his merit, his satisfaction, his victory over death flow into us. The white-red tide of grace and glory from his wounded heart never ebbs; everything is for participation or cooperation. This is Catholicism in its deepest meaning: life in, with and through Christ.

St Paul says that Christians can share in Christ's sufferings, make up what is lacking in his afflictions for the sake of his Mystical Body (cf. Col. 1:24). In other words, by the grace of the Head, the members of the Mystical Body are called, in faith and charity, to unite their sufferings to the perfect self-offering of Christ, who in his Passion somehow made all human pain his own. And by their share in his Passion, Christians do something for their brethren in the Church.

What of the Descent into Hell? Can Christians in this life be said to share in any way in the Holy Saturday mystery? St Thomas, in his exposition of the Apostles' Creed, suggests that they can.

> Christ went down into Hell for our salvation, and we should be careful frequently to go down there too.[80]

This spiritual descent is realized in two ways: first, by regular meditation on Hell as an arm and aid against sin; secondly, by Masses, prayers, and almsgiving to help the holy souls in that region of the underworld we call Purgatory.

Adrienne and Balthasar go further. They envisage the possibility of certain souls in this life being given the grace to taste something of the Lord's experience in Sheol, not as an end in itself, but in order, in and through Christ the Conqueror of Hades, to assist their brethren in the Church, to aid those who find themselves plunged into the black hole of depression, doubt, confusion, despair.

Clearly, the servant's experience of Hell will be very different from that of the Master. "No creature can ever be ranked alongside the incarnate Word and Redeemer".[81] However closely conformed the Christian is to Christ, the unlikeness between them is always greater.[82] The most Christlike of the saints have been those most acutely aware of the distance between their little crosses and the great Cross of the Lord.[83] When asked, in this life, to go into Hell with Christ, the saints know that, by their sins, they deserve to be there, while he is the guiltless Son of God, descending, not by desert but, vicariously, by the purest and freest love for us and his Father.

We may be allowed into the Lord's Passion, even into his Hell, but this paradox is inescapable: I suffer with him, but he at the same time suffers for me.[84]

The only way to union with the Trinity, with the Father in the Spirit, is Jesus, the incarnate and crucified Son. We must share in his sufferings if we are to know the power of his resurrection. The "purgative way" is nothing other than the way of the Cross. As St John of the Cross says, since Christ reconciled the human race to his Father at the moment of his own abandonment by the Father, we cannot be brought to union with God without "the living, sensory and

127

spiritual, exterior and interior death of the cross".[85] This is a law, not of suffering, but of love. The Son-Bridegroom invites the soul to join him in that adventure of love, for the Father and all mankind, which took him first to the Cross and then into Hell. So, in the dark night of the spirit, the soul seems to "see Hell and perdition open before it". She is the one who, as the Psalmist says, "goes down into Sheol alive" (Ps. 54:16). She endures on earth the purgation that would otherwise be endured in the life to come.[86]

Many holy people have been given a mystical share in the Lord's Descent into Hell. According to Adrienne, this was the true meaning of the "dark night" of St John of the Cross, that total "living death" of which we have just spoken: "The night of John of the Cross is much more a night of Holy Saturday than of the Cross". She admits that St John himself did not interpret it in this way. "He fixes his eyes so much on the crucified Lord that he sees the Crucified's non-vision, but not what is revealed to the Lord in this non-seeing". St Teresa of Avila, in her autobiography, tells us how the Lord plunged her into Hell so that she could see with her own eyes "the place from which his mercy had delivered [her]". The experience enkindled in Teresa an apostolic zeal to save souls; to free just one soul from these torments, she was ready to die a multitude of deaths. Similarly, the Russian Orthodox Staretz Silouan of Mount Athos, who died in 1938, was told by the Lord when he prayed for mercy in the midst of demonic temptation: "Keep your mind in Hell, and do not despair".[87]

The Holy Saturday mystery stood at the very centre of the spiritual and theological mission of Adrienne von Speyr. Balthasar tells us that when her Holy Week experiences began, he expected her suffering to cease with the death of the Lord on Good Friday afternoon. In fact, after a brief pause, corresponding to the deposition of the good thief in Paradise, she had the sudden feeling of "crashing to the bottom of the abyss".[88] There was no physical pain, just the loss of all contact with other human beings and with God. Faith, hope, and charity seemed unattainable, dereliction absolute.

I repeat that this anguish, this night, is not something to be sought for its own sake. It is not beautiful. It is ugly and terrible. But when borne humbly, with a faith that is childlike and a love that wants to spend itself, it can, by the grace of the risen Lord, do great good for the Church. In particular, through the Spirit by whom we live and coinhere in the Mystical Body, it can relieve all whose hearts are desperate.

Critique and Assessment

Magnificent and inspiring though it is, Balthasar's theology of the Descent in many ways bewilders me. Two years before his death he wrote a book to defend the orthodoxy of his views on Hell and took the trouble of obtaining an imprimatur from the Cardinal Prefect of the Holy Office. Nonetheless, despite all the painstaking and scholarly qualifications and explanations, he does give the impression to some of his readers that Christ's Descent makes univeral salvation inevitable. For example, at the 1985 Rome symposium, he explained how on Holy Saturday Adrienne experienced total lonelines.

And yet here, in this Christian, indeed christological loneliness, lies hope for the person who refusing all love, damns himself. This man who wants to be totally alone, will he not after all find beside him Someone still lonelier, the Son forsaken by the Father, who will prevent (*hindern*) him from experiencing his self-chosen Hell to the end?[89]

129

When I first read this, it disturbed me, because it seemed to imply the possibility of a conversion taking place in the Hell of the damned. I cannot think that that is what Balthasar means. No, what he is describing is the Hound of Heaven's loving pursuit of the self-destructive soul to the very end *of this life*, revealing his presence to him in the loneliness of an earthly Hell, for no one has descended more deeply than he.

There is no mechanical Origenistic universalism in Balthasar. He wants simply to assert the Christian's right and duty to hope and to pray for the final salvation of all men. We are not all given the grace to share mystically in Christ's Descent into Hell, but there is still much we can do to cooperate with the Conqueror of Hades.

> We can re-animate the spirit of solidarity in our lives, that capacity to bear the burden of other people with them, praying with fervour – and prayer of that kind is infallible – that our brothers and sisters be not finally lost. Doing penance is a particularly effective way of attaining this. Mary has been recommending it to us for years in Medjugorje.

Perhaps the most difficult notion in Balthasar's theology of the Descent is the idea of Christ viewing "sin without sinners". It is hard to see what this could mean. Sin, like all evil, has no substance of its own. It exists only as the disorder in a free creaturely action. To this objection, I think it could be replied on Balthasar's behalf that Christ's *visio peccati* in Hell is intellectual, not ocular. It is not the sensory perception of a material object, but the recognition by the soul of the dead Jesus of what sin amounts to and where it finally leads to, the second death, eternal perdition. This reply, too, raises difficulties, because sin, as privative, cannot, strictly speaking, be an

130

object of knowledge, for only what is, is knowable. Sin can only be known as qualifying concrete voluntary actions. The *mysterium iniquitatis*, unlike the *mysterium deitatis*, is mystery by way of defect, not excess, of intelligibility. And yet perhaps that is the point: in Hell the immaculate soul of Jesus looks into the yawning gulf of sin's unmeaning. In death, which came into the world through sin, he sees creaturely wickedness in all its destructive futility. He has always known it was so, but now, in Sheol, he sees it as overcome by his Sacrifice on the Cross; the lie is exposed, the nothingness unmasked.

And what of the "effigies", those bas-reliefs of sinful persons uncovered by Christ in Hell? My own hunch is that this is a way of saying that sin depersonalizes. Human persons only find their fulfilment through union with the incarnate divine person of the Word, and through him with the Father in the Holy Spirit. Sinfully to turn from the Creator to the creature is to prefer things to the Three-Personed source of all personhood, to exchange, in St Paul's words, "the glory of the immortal God for images resembling mortal man or birds or animals or reptiles" (Rom. 1:23). Interestingly, the apostle speaks of the sinful "works" of the flesh in contrast to the "fruits" of the Spirit (Gal. 5:19), as if the vices make men mechanical, while the virtues release them into spontaneous flowering. Satan, ontologically, is a real personal entity, a fallen angel, and yet, as both Ratzinger and Balthasar have argued, since he is definitively not *in Christo*, he is an "unperson", lacking the positive qualities of personal flourishing that only the grace of Christ can give.[90]

So, then, we can begin to see what Adrienne means when she says that the effigies are what sinners give to sin from their own substance. Here is the "unadmirable exchange" of human iniquity: the impersonal and insubstantial becomes personal; the personal becomes impersonal.

A Message for our Times

Despite my puzzles, I am convinced that this account of the Descent into Hell is of enormous importance, not only theologically but apologetically. As Wilhelm Maas has said, the present time is especially favourable for receiving it, for so many people of our century, in their lifetime on earth, have experienced the apparent absence of God, desolation, depression. Hell is an exact description of the life on earth of many human beings today. The great writers of the last hundred years, both Christian and non-Christian, have testified to it: Baudelaire, Rimbaud, Kafka, Claudel, Bernanos, Le Fort, Sartre, Solzhenitsyn.[91] There is nowhere God has not been, no depth of Godforsakenness which he has not explored in person, no darkness into which he has not poured light. However deep we may feel we have descended, God made man has descended more deeply, so even "if I descend into Hell, thou art there also" (Ps. 138:8).

> We must recall today that there is a drama in Christ which is deeper than every possible Hell that a human being might experience: abandonment of the Son of God by the Father, who is his eternal beatitude and sustenance.[92]

I mentioned above that the Descent into Hell seems to have been specially important to St Peter. Might this not be because, after the Resurrection, he learnt that, while he was in his hell of remorse (those terrible hours from his denial on the Thursday night to the Resurrection on Easter Sunday), his Lord and Master, for love of him, was in Sheol, bearing his and all human hopelessness?

Dying and death, the very deadness of Sheol, have been made his own by God the Son, in his human soul, out of loving obedience to the Father. Even upon the absence of God, he has printed the sign of the Son, the filial sign of the Cross. The prison has been made a way: the wasteland of dereliction has been transformed into a royal highway, a track through the trackless waste, the road to the Father's house and heart.

9
GLORIOUS MYSTERIES

Lady Day and Easter Day

Without the Resurrection, the other March mysteries would be of no avail. Indeed, if Christ is not risen, our whole faith is in vain (cf. 1 Cor. 15:14). No Easter, no Christianity.[1] "Without the Resurrection", says Balthasar, "the whole Trinitarian plan of salvation would be incomprehensible, and the work begun in the life of Jesus would remain meaningless".[2] Lady Day and all that follows it would have no meaning without Easter Sunday. But the converse is also true: Easter Sunday makes no sense without Lady Day. The Resurrection does not undo the Incarnation. For it is the Father's raising up of the Son in the flesh taken from the Virgin (*secundum carnem*, says the Roman Canon on Easter Day). It was in his Virgin-born body, the body scourged and spat upon, nailed and pierced and laid in the tomb, that the Son of God rose from the dead. It was changed, wonderfully transformed, but in state, not in nature. It was the very same body not only in its subject and by continuity of form, but in essence and in number. Balthasar states this as the fundamental principle of his theology of the Resurrection: the Risen One is the Crucified One.[3]

The soul in which Christ descended into Sheol was not left there by the Father, nor was his flesh allowed to see corruption (cf. Acts 2:27f.). On Easter Sunday the Father raised up the Son in the wholeness of his

human nature – his body from the grave, his soul from
Hades. The risen Lord is not a ghost but an indestruct-
ibly alive, *complete* human being (Luke 24:39). It is
important to state this clearly because of the widespread modern heresy that the emptiness of the tomb
is irrelevant to the doctrine of the Resurrection, that
Our Lord is resurrected in his soul alone, or in the
minds of his disciples, or in some kind of replacement
body. Balthasar regards these denials of the bodily
Resurrection as a revival of Gnostic dualism, for they
imply a subtle contempt for the material order and its
capacity for transfiguration. As Balthasar says, referring to Christ's risen body, "from Valentinus [the
Gnostic] to Bultmann, people have tried to spiritualize
and demythologize this flesh and blood".[4] Biblical
revelation just cannot be etherealized. The glory of the
risen Jesus is visible, tangible, corporeal.

> Being raised up in the Spirit, to the sphere of the
> divine, in the Resurrection of the flesh, does not
> mean being "spiritualized".[5]

The body is not an optional extra for man, as if, as
Plato imagined, the self could be identified with the
spiritual soul. No, St Thomas says, reasserting
Biblical-Christian anthropology, "my soul is not my
self".[6] The person is the possessor of the complete
nature of the species, body as well as soul.[7] A person
who is dead, one whose immortal soul is separated
from his body, is strictly speaking, on the Thomist
view, not a man but a dead man.[8] If God had left his
Son's body behind in the tomb, Jesus would have
ceased to be perfect man, fully and completely
human. What God the Son assumed on Lady Day was
not laid aside on Easter Day. Even during the three
days of death, when his body and soul were separated
from one another, each remained hypostatically
united to his divine person; they continued to be his

very own.[9] As the great Welsh poet, D. Gwenallt Jones, says:

> He did not fling our bit of flesh like a rag on the rubbish-dump of Gehenna,
> Or throw our blood there like a bottle of worn-out medicine,
> But raised them from the grip of the worms' incomparable three days,
> A transparent spiritual body, the perfection of man and God.[10]

The flesh and blood which his Mother gave him with unbounded virginal faith and love was not cast into corruption, but flooded with glory, with the power of the Spirit. So much does he love us, so precious to him is our humanity, that when he assumes it, God the Son does not absorb it, and when he rises, he does not reject it.

The Objectivity of the Resurrection

The trend of Liberal Protestantism from Schleiermacher to Bultmann is to reduce the Resurrection to a purely subjective experience on the part of the disciples, a new attitude to Jesus and his Cross. Balthasar joins his friend Karl Barth in firmly resisting this existential reduction: the Lord has really risen (verily (ontôs), says St Luke (cf. 24:34)).[11] The Resurrection has a real objectivity: it is something which first of all happens to the body of Jesus and only in the second place, precisely as the glorious reality it is, has a transforming effect on the minds and hearts of the disciples.

> He did not come as a projection of his disciples' living faith, for he came when not one of them had the slightest belief in that possibility.[12]

136

The evangelists present the disciples in an unflatter-
ing light. When the Lord, before the event, predicted
his Resurrection, they did not understand him and
discussed among themselves what "rising from the
dead" could mean (cf. Mark 9:10). The eschatology
and apocalyptic of the tradition in which they had
been brought up offered no help. It looked forward to
the general resurrection at the end of history but knew
nothing of an anticipated or proleptic resurrection. In
the Resurrection of Jesus, says Balthasar, the eschatology of the Old Testament itself dies and rises again; it
is fulfilled by being shattered.[13] No, as St Ignatius of
Antioch argues, writing on the road to Rome and
certain death, only the objective, real, bodily Resurrection of Jesus can explain the transformation of
craven and confused men into martyrs.[14] Of course,
the Resurrection is not a "bare fact", something you
can take or leave. It is a fact that calls for conversion,
real, not notional assent. It is an event without
analogy, the Event of events, the defining centre of all
history.[15]

The Resurrection and the Trinity

> The Resurrection is a Trinitarian event . . . it is the
> Father who, as "the God of the living" (Rom. 4:17)
> awakens the Son from among the dead so that he,
> as one freshly united with the Father, can send forth
> God's Spirit into the Church.[16]

The Resurrection is the Father's response to the Son's
obedience unto death, the paternal acceptance of the
filial Sacrifice.[17] It is God the Father who takes the
initiative as Creator, for the Resurrection of his Son is
the fulfilment of his creative work.[18] He reveals
himself as the faithful God of Abraham, Isaac, and

Jacob, the steadfast God of the covenant (cf. Rom. 4:17ff.).[19] Resurrecting Jesus corporeally and integrally, the Father shows him in his glory to the world, enthrones him as Pantocrator.[20] Here is the answer to the prayer of the Son before his Passon: "Father, glorify thou me in thy own presence with the glory which I had with thee before the world was made" (John 17:5).

The Resurrection is the work of the whole Trinity, each Person exercising the one divine power in the manner appropriate to him. It is, therefore, the Son's and the Spirit's as well as the Father's. It is in the Spirit that the Father raises Jesus from the dead (cf. Rom. 8:11). And "though the idea of a dead man bringing himself back to life is a strange one, it must nonetheless be said that Jesus – whose death was a work of his vibrantly living love, a love that was one with the divine Spirit of love – is also involved in the return to life."[21]

The sending of the Spirit from the Father by the ascended Son completes the Easter mystery. Only when Jesus has been glorified can the Paraclete be given (cf. John 7:39). Despite the differences of their time-scales, Luke and John agree that the Son goes to the Father so that the Spirit may come upon the Church.

> The reunion of the Father with the Son (in his human nature!) as a single (economic) principle of spiration [is] the precondition for the (economic) sending forth of the Spirit into the Church and the redeemed world.[22]

As we have already noted several times, Balthasar emphasizes that the Holy Spirit is the Spirit of the Son as well as of the Father, the Spirit of the incarnate Word, possessed by him "without measure", flowing from, always returning to, his glorious manhood. The

Third Person of the Trinity is never, therefore, a Spirit of disincarnation. He is inseparable from the flesh and blood of the risen Jesus. When Jesus breathes the Spirit on the apostles, they feel themselves sensibly touched.

> . . . the Church assembled at Easter encounters a Spirit-filled but also corporeal Christ: he breathes his Spirit into them (John 20:22), but he also wants to be touched by them so that no one will think that he is "a spirit" (Luke 24:39).[23]

In the Farewell Discourse, when Our Lord says that he must go so that he may return with a new kind of intimacy in the Spirit (cf. John 14:18ff.), he is speaking of his presence, in his incarnate reality, in the Church and her sacraments, the Eucharist above all.[24] The water (Baptism), the blood (Eucharist), and the Spirit are always found together (cf. 1 John 5:7).[25] The Spirit is the "Lord of the sacraments", the *Creator Spiritus* who effects the miracle of transubstantiation and all the other mysteries in which the Son sanctifies men through his manhood.[26]

The Spirit of the risen Lord is always placing the Church anew under the sign of the Cross. In the Acts of the Apostles, the infant Church is truly an Easter people, yet facing at every moment persecution and violent hatred. "Easter occurs on earth, but it does not lead away from the Cross but always to it".[27]

> The Spirit is not bestowed before the *Triduum Paschale* (Jn. 7:39). When his mission is "accomplished", Jesus "breathes out" his Spirit and gives him back to the Father (Lk. 23:46; cf. Mk. 15:37; Mt. 27:50; Jn. 19:30); then, when he is risen, as disposer of the Spirit, he breathes him into the Church (Jn. 20:22), the Spirit, both sevenfold and single, of suffering and of resurrection, who leads all who

139

follow Jesus into a wholly new form of dramatic existence.[28]

The Forty Days

The Forty Days from Easter Sunday to Ascension Thursday are the time when the Lord shows himself to his disciples as truly human, even homely. "Any suggestion of 'seeing ghosts' is quietly, almost humorously, set aside" (cf. Luke 24:39).[29] Although he visits and leaves them with a new resurrection subtlety, though there is an initial, mysterious non-recognition, his meetings with the disciples "have all the ease and naturalness of human relationships, they hear and see one another, touch one another, eat together, and the historical character of the whole is taken for granted".[30] He eats bread and fish with them (cf. Luke 24:42f.; John 21:12–13), something remembered by Peter in his preaching (cf. Acts 10:41) and by Ignatius of Antioch seventy-five or so years later.[31]

> All these events are so many unmistakable testimonies to the fact that the risen Christ and the apostolic witnesses exist contemporaneously in the same time.[32]

According to Balthasar, the forty days – genuine earthly time yet filled with a blessed and death-conquered spaciousness – are sacramental, ecclesial days.

> We shall take as our first principle that Christ's existence, and hence his mode of duration in the Eucharist and the sacraments, is, as far as concerns himself, no different from that which belongs to the forty days . . . The new element of difference is only

that whereas during the forty days he lets this companionship appear openly as fulfilment, in the time of the Church it happens in concealment under the sacramental forms. But the forty days were expressly intended as an introduction and initiation of the days of the Church.[33]

When Jesus appears, it is for the sake of a mission in the Church. (This makes the depiction of the appearances in the choir of Notre Dame in Paris particularly appropriate.) Mary Magdalene is sent with a message for the apostles (cf. John 20:17). Her personal and human love is being enlarged, becoming Catholic.[34] Luke pictures Jesus giving the disciples instruction about Scripture and the Kingdom (Luke 24:44ff.; Acts 1:3, 8). Matthew shows him sending them off to exercise the ministry of word and sacrament (28:10ff.). John links the mission of the apostles with the Son's own Trinitarian mission (20:21). Their apostolic office is a participation in and extension of the mission of the Son. Then there is Peter's initiation into a primacy uniting office with love (John 21:15ff.).[35]

The Resurrection and the Eucharist

For Balthasar, the risen body of Jesus is Eucharistic, immortally alive and therefore permanently available in its sacrificial givenness. The Father has not withdrawn the gift of his Son in our human nature.

It is essential that the [precious] wounds enter into the Resurrection and Glorification. This is not just to prove to the disciples that the tortured body is identical with the body spiritualized beyond their comprehension, the body that can walk through closed doors. No, the point is even more fundamental: his broken-open-ness . . . his flesh bound-

141

lessly distributed, his blood poured out, enables them to partake of the essential infinitude of his divine person.[36]

It is precisely the Resurrection which makes possible, in the power of the Spirit, our Eucharistic access to the drama of Christ's Passion and thus to a salvific sharing in his sufferings and the power of his resurrection (cf. Phil. 3:10).

The Assumption of Our Lady: Easter in August

The Christian hope is for the redemption of the whole person, not just a spiritual "life everlasting" but the resurrection of the body. This general resurrection, which comes at the end of history, has been already inaugurated in the Resurrection of Jesus, our Head. He is the first fruits of those who have fallen asleep (1 Cor. 15:20). Thus ours at the end will be nothing other than the extension to us of Christ's own resurrection.[37] He will then conform our lowly bodies to be like his glorious body (cf. Phil. 3:21).[38] This bodily glorification depends on our communion, corporeal as well as spiritual, with Jesus. "He who eats my flesh and drinks my blood has eternal life, and I will raise him up at the last day" (John 6:54). Since he is the Resurrection and the Life, whoever lives and believes in him will never die (cf. John 11:25). No one lives and believes in Jesus more deeply than Mary. She in love gave him human life, in faith gave him flesh. And so it was she who, when her earthly course was ended, was the first to receive his risen glory in body as well as soul. The transfiguration of the material cosmos, the renewal of creation, is inaugurated not only in the body united hypostatically to the divine person of the

142

Son but also in the body of the human person of his Mother, "the body that made him a man, the earthly kingdom prepared for God".[39] She who received him on earth from Heaven was received by him into Heaven from earth.[40] Mary's glorified body, inseparable from that of her Son, "contains within itself the promise that all flesh, longing now for redemption, will be saved".[41] *Maria assumpta* is first of the totally redeemed and thus the sign of hope for all the struggling sufferers who shelter beneath her mantle. She is God incarnate's own pledge that the divinization which he brings to men, by his saving March mysteries, is not the destruction of their humanity but its fulfilment.

> I am all at once what Christ is, since he was what I
>   am, and
> This Jack, joke, poor potsherd, matchwood, immor-
>   tal diamond,
>   Is immortal diamond.[42]

ENDSPIEL

The world's recreation began one March nineteen-hundred and ninety years ago and ends at the End – when the Virgin's Son will come again in glory to judge the living and the dead. Hans Urs von Balthasar has placed his great knowledge in the hands of the Church to help her sons and daughters understand more deeply this whole great drama of God's love from Genesis to the Gospels to the Apocalypse. The last time I saw him was on the Solemnity of the Ascension one month before his death. He celebrated Holy Mass and preached, speaking beautifully of the hope we have that where the Head has gone in the fullness of our human nature the members will follow. He mentioned a strange and beautiful idea of St Augustine's, that the Church is a tree, with its roots in Heaven, growing down towards earth. Let us pray for the great soul of Hans Urs von Balthasar and for ourselves that we with him, by God's mercy, may reach our heavenly roots in the company of Mary, John, Ignatius, and all the saints of God.

ABBREVIATIONS

The Works of Hans Urs von Balthasar

AC   *Au coeur du mystère rédempteur* (Paris, 1980).

ARA   *Der antirömische Affekt: Wie lässt sich das Papsttum in der Gesamtkirche integrieren* (Freiburg, 1974).

C   *Cordula oder der Ernstfall* (Einsiedeln, 1967).

CM   *Christlich meditieren* (Freiburg, 1984).

Credo   *Credo: Meditationen zum Apostolischen Glaubensbekenntnis* (Freiburg, 1989).

CS   *The Christian State of Life*, ET (San Francisco, 1983).

DK   *Du krönst das Jahr mit deiner Huld: Radiopredigten* (Einsiedeln, 1982).

E   *Elucidations*, ET (London, 1975).

Ep   *Epilog* (Einsiedeln & Trier, 1987).

FG   *First Glance at Adrienne von Speyr*, ET (San Francisco, 1981).

GL 1   *The Glory of the Lord: A Theological Aesthetics*, 1: Seeing the Form, ET (Edinburgh, 1982).

GL 2   *The Glory of the Lord: A Theological Aesthetics*, 2: Studies in Theological Style: Clerical Styles, ET (Edinburgh, 1984).

GL 3   *The Glory of the Lord: A Theological Aesthetics*, 3: Studies in Theological Style: Lay Styles, ET (Edinburgh, 1986).

H 3/1/1   *Herrlichkeit: Eine theologische Ästhetik*, vol.

	III/1: Im Raum der Metaphysik, 1. Altertum, 2nd edition (Einsiedeln, 1975).
H 3/1/2	*Herrlichkeit: Eine theologische Ästhetik*, vol. III/1: Im Raum der Metaphysik, 2. Neuzeit, 2nd edition (Einsiedeln, 1975).
H 3/2/2	*Herrlichkeit: Eine theologische Ästhetik*, vol. III/2/2: Neuer Bund (Einsiedeln, 1969).
KL	*Kosmische Liturgie: Das Weltbild Maximus des Bekenners* (Einsiedeln, 1961).
MH	*Maria für heute* (Freiburg, 1987).
MP	*Mysterium Paschale* in *Mysterium Salutis: Grundriss heilsgeschichtlicher Dogmatik III/2*, ed. J. Feiner & M. Löhrer (Einsiedeln, Zürich, & Cologne, 1969), pp. 133–326.
MPE	(with Joseph Ratzinger) *Marie première Église*, FT (Paris, 1981).
NE	*New Elucidations*, ET (San Francisco, 1986).
PI	*Pneuma und Institution: Skizzen zur Theologie IV* (Einsiedeln, 1974).
SpC	*Spiritus Creator: Skizzen zur Theologie III* (Einsiedeln, 1967).
SP	*A Short Primer for Unsettled Laymen*, ET (San Francisco, 1985).
SV	*Sponsa Verbi: Skizzen zur Theologie II* (Einsiedeln, 1960).
Symp	*Adrienne von Speyr und ihre kirchliche Sendung: Akten des römischen Symposiums 27–29 September 1952*, ed. H.U.v. Balthasar and others (Einsiedeln, 1986).
TD 1	*Theodramatik*, vol. I: Prolegomena (Einsiedeln, 1973).
TD 2/1	*Theodramatik*, vol. II: Die Personen des Spiels, part 1: Der Mensch in Gott (Einsiedeln, 1976).
TD 2/2	*Theodramatik*, vol. II: Die Personen des Spiels, part 2: Die Personen in Christus (Einsiedeln, 1978).

TD 3	*Theodramatik*, vol. III: Die Handlung (Einsiedeln, 1980).
TD 4	*Theodramatik*, vol. IV: Das Endspiel (Einsiedeln, 1983).
TG	*The Threefold Garland: The World's Salvation in Mary's Prayer*, ET (San Francisco, 1982).
TH	*A Theology of History*, ET (London and Sydney, 1970).
TL 1	*Theologik*, vol. I: Wahrheit der Welt (Einsiedeln, 1985).
TL 2	*Theologik*, vol. II: Wahrheit Gottes (Einsiedeln, 1985).
TL 3	*Theologik*, vol. III: Der Geist der Wahrheit (Einsiedeln, 1987).
UA	*Unser Auftrag: Bericht und Entwurf* (Einsiedeln, 1984).
VC	*Verbum Caro: Skizzen zur Theologie I* (Einsiedeln, 1960).
WS	*Die Wahrheit ist symphonisch: Aspekte des christlichen Pluralismus* (Einsiedeln, 1972).

The Works of Adrienne von Speyr

AH 1	*Das Allerheiligenbuch*, part 1 (Einsiedeln, 1966).
Conf	*Confession*, ET (San Francisco, 1985).
EH	*Erde und Himmel: Ein Tagebuch*, 3 volumes (Einsiedeln, 1975–1976) (references in the text are to the volume number and paragraph number).
HL	*Handmaid of the Lord*, ET (San Francisco, 1985).
JK	*Betrachtungen über das Johannesevangelium* (references to volume number and page number).

1. *Das Word wird Fleisch* (ch. 1–5) (Einsiedeln, 1949).
2. *Die Streitreden* (ch. 6–12) (Einsiedeln, 1949).
3. *Die Abschiedsreden* (ch. 13–17) (Einsiedeln, 1948).
4. *Geburt der Kirche* (ch. 18–21) (Einsiedeln, 1949).

KH 1   *Kreuz und Hölle*, part 1: Die Passionen (Einsiedeln, 1966).

KH 2   *Kreuz und Hölle*, part 2: Die Auftragshöllen (Einsiedeln, 1972).

LB   *Das Licht und die Bilder: Elemente der Kontemplation* (Einsiedeln, 1955).

ME   *Maria in der Erlösung* (Einsiedeln, 1979).

OM   *Das Wort und die Mystik*, part 2: Objektive Mystik (Einsiedeln, 1970).

TdG   *Theologie der Geschlechter* (Einsiedeln, 1969).

WP   *The World of Prayer* (San Francisco, 1985).

Studies of Balthasar's Theology

Bätzing   Georg Bätzing, *Die Eucharistie als Opfer der Kirche nach Hans Urs von Balthasar* (Einsiedeln, 1986).

Löser   Werner Löser, *Im Geiste des Origenes: Hans Urs von Balthasar als Interpret der Theologie der Kirchenväter* (Frankfurt, 1976).

Marchesi   Giovanni Marchesi SJ, *La cristologia di Hans Urs von Balthasar: La figura di Gesù Cristo espressione visibile di Dio* (Rome, 1977).

Miscellaneous Abbreviations

CCSL   *Corpus Christianorum, Series Latina* (Turnhout, 1953ff).

CICR   *Communio: International Catholic Review* (Notre Dame, Indiana).

CSCO   *Corpus Scriptorum Christianorum Orientalium* (Paris, 1903ff).

DS   H. Denzinger & A. Schönmetzer, *Enchiridion Symbolorum*, 36th ed. (Rome, 1976).

ET   English translation.

FT   French translation.

GIRM   *General Instruction on the Roman Missal, 1970* in *Vatican Council II: The Conciliar and Post-Conciliar Documents*, ed. A. Flannery (Dublin, 1975), pp. 154–205.

IKZ   *Internationale katholische Zeitschrift: Communio* (Cologne).

In Jo.   St Thomas Aquinas, *Lectura super Johannem*.

In symb. St Thomas Aquinas, *Collationes super Credo in Deum*.

LG   Vatican II, Dogmatic Constitution on the Church, *Lumen Gentium*, in *Sacrosanctum Oecumenicum Vaticanum II: Constitutiones, Decreta, Declarationes* (Vatican City, 1966).

Maas   Wilhelm Maas, *Gott und die Hölle: Studien zum Descensus Christi* (Einsiedeln, 1979).

OR   *L'Osservatore Romano* (Vatican City).

PG   *Patrologia Graeca*, ed. J.P. Migne (Paris, 1857ff).

PL   *Patrologia Latina*, ed. J.P. Migne (Paris, 1844ff).

RM   Pope John Paul II, *Redemptoris Mater*, ET (Catholic Truth Society, London, 1987).

SC   *Sources chrétiennes* (Paris, 1940ff).

ST   St Thomas Aquinas, *Summa Theologiae*.

NOTES

Introduction

[1] Cf. the *Adversus Judaeos* attributed to Tertullian (8; PL 2.656). By the same ancient reckoning, 25th March is also the date of Adam's creation and Fall. A medieval author enlaced the four anniversaries in three lines of undistinguished Latin verse:

> Salva festa dies, quae vulnera nostra coerces,
>> Angelus est missus, est passus et in cruce Christus,
> Est Adam factus, et eodem lapsus
>> (*Summa Aurea* vol. I (Paris, 1862), p. 602).

Even when Easter is late and Good Friday is not strictly a mystery of March, the Annunciation still falls deep within Lent, the season when the Church thinks specially of the Cross.

[2] *Des heiligen Ephraem des Syrers Hymnen de Nativitate (Epiphania)*, tr. E. Beck, CSCO, *Scriptores Syri* (Louvain, 1959), p. 83.

[3] H. Grierson (ed.), *The Poems of John Donne* (London, 1933), p. 305. Donne's "Holy Sonnets" show his appreciation of the unity of the *mysteria vitae Jesu*: the last line of the first sonnet is repeated as the first line of the next, and so on, from "Annunciation" to "Ascension", the seven forming a "crown of prayer and praise" (ibid., pp. 289–292). Donne was fascinated by the reconciliation of opposites and all surprising unities.

This is why maps attracted him "as devices for making contraries meet" (John Carey, *John Donne* (London, 1981), p. 264).

4 "If reason, illumined by faith, inquires earnestly, piously, and soberly, it attains, by God's grace (*Deo dante*), a certain understanding of the mysteries, which is most fruitful, both by analogy with the things it knows naturally, and from the connection of the mysteries with one another (*e mysteriorum ipsorum nexu inter se*) and with man's ultimate end" (DS 3016).

5 *Katholikos* from *kata holou* or *kath' holou* ("on the whole", "generally speaking"). See the classic study by Henri de Lubac SJ, Balthasar's mentor, *Catholicisme: Les aspects sociaux du dogme* (Paris, 1938), pp. 23f. Balthasar twice translated this work.

6 *Catecheses* 18, 23; PG 33, 1044A.

7 See Balthasar's own little book on Catholicity: *Katholisch: Aspekte des Mysteriums* (Einsiedeln, 1975), passim.

8 Pope John Paul II said of him at the consistory: "Alas, as you have all learned with great sadness, the Lord God, by the mysterious design of his providence, has meanwhile called to himself Hans Urs von Balthasar, an outstanding man and most eminent theologian, whom we would very gladly have seen numbered among the Cardinals and lavished with our congratulations and marks of esteem. He has been snatched from us by an unexpected death, and we recommend him therefore to the goodness of the merciful redeemer, that as a reward for his merits on earth, for his long life of sacred study and of teaching, he may grant him, in exchange for this cardinalatial dignity which he did not live to receive, the rewards of Heaven, which are better, richer and more certain" (OR (1988), n. 27, p. 1).

⁹ TL 1, p. viii. This is another Johannine trait in Balthasar. In *Cordula*, he says that the evangelist "argues in circular fashion" (94).

¹⁰ UA, pp. 103f. The holistic "norm for theology" is God's revelation of himself in Christ as articulated in the Creed, the *regula fidei*: ". . . the Trinity of God (in the threefold structure of the Creed), Creation, Incarnation by the Spirit in Mary, the Passion and Resurrection *pro nobis*, his role as judge, the Holy Spirit and his work, namely, the one Church (with Scripture, ministry, tradition, and communion), the sacraments (Eucharist and Baptism are mentioned), the resurrection of man in his totality, and the goal, eternal life in God" (*L'Heure de l'Église*, 107f. For similar statements on the need for theology to reflect the Trinitarian wholeness of the Creed, see TD 4, pp. 11f; Ep 50).

¹¹ "Catholics must listen to those who point out a piece of the totality of faith which is missing or not sufficiently realized. On the other hand, a member of the Catholic Church must be aware that his 'separated brothers' can alert him only to things that have always rested in the fullness of his faith, things which were merely lost or forgotten through negligence or guilt. If this guilt is admitted, the claim to Catholic totality is possible without arrogance" (SP 119).

¹² ARA, pp. 115ff. On the notion of the "Christological Constellation", see J. Saward, "Mary and Peter in the Christological Constellation: Balthasar's Ecclesiology" in J. Riches (ed.). *The Analogy of Beauty: The Theology of Hans Urs von Balthasar* (Edinburgh, 1986), pp. 105–133; and Bätzing, pp. 59–61.

¹³ FG p. 13. On the inseparability of his work and hers, see UA pp. 11f.

¹⁴ FG pp. 64ff.; UA pp. 81f.

[15] On *Gestalt* see GL 1, passim; H 3/1/1, pp. 29–39; Marchesi, pp. 17–33 and passim. For an excellent introduction to Balthasar's theological aesthetics, see the two articles by M. Waldstein in *Communio*: "Hans Urs von Balthasar's Theological Aesthetics", *Communio* 11 (1984), pp. 4–27; and "Von Balthasar's *The Glory of the Lord*", *Communio* 14 (1987), pp. 12–33.

[16] On Christ as the "centre of the form of revelation", see GL 1, pp. 463–525.

[17] On the dramatic character of the aesthetic, see TD 1, pp. 15–22; TD 2/1, pp. 18–33.

[18] "To be transported . . . belongs to the very origin of Christianity" (GL 1, p. 33).

[19] On the interdependence of the three parts of Balthasar's trilogy (the Theological Aesthetic, the Theodramatic, and the Theologic), see especially TL 1, pp. vii–xxi and Ep, passim.

[20] On *Sich-zeigen*, *Sich-geben*, and *Sich-sagen*, see Ep pp. 45ff.

[21] Cf. TH p. 89. On the notion of Christ as the *universale concretum*, see Marchesi, pp. 33ff.

[22] On "Truth as Fullness", see TL 2, pp. 20–23.

[23] Jesus is "the concretion of the Triune God" (ARA, pp. 112f.). The office of Peter is "the concretion of Christ" (ARA, pp. 136ff.).

[24] Henri de Lubac, "A Witness of Christ in the Church: Hans Urs von Balthasar", CICR (1975), p. 230.

[25] WS, p. 13. On the "universality of the Catholic" in Balthasar, see Löser, pp. 50f.

[26] GL 2 and GL 3 are devoted to the "clerical styles" and "lay styles" respectively.

[27] Preaching at his funeral Mass, Cardinal Ratzinger described him as a "real teacher of the faith, a pointer to the source of living water, a witness to the Word, someone from whom we can learn about

Christ" ("Homilie beim Gedenkgottesdienst für Hans Urs von Balthasar", IKZ 17 (1988), p. 476).

1 Lady Day and Good Friday

1. *Angelo nuntiante, et Spiritu Sancto adveniente, mox Verbum in utero, mox intra uterum Verbum caro* (St Gregory the Great, cited by St Thomas Aquinas, ST 3a 33, 1). For Balthasar's interpretation of the Annunciation, see TG pp. 27–34.
2. MP p. 142; H 3/2/2, p. 197.
3. MP p. 140.
4. St Athanasius, *Epistola ad Epictetum* 6–7; PG 26.1061A; St Leo the Great, *Sermo* 71, 2; PL 54.387.
5. MP p. 142.
6. MP p. 185.
7. See his comments on the book on the Thomist/Scotist debate by R. Haubst, *Vom Sinn der Menschwerdung* (Munich, 1969) (TD 2/2, p. 232). St Thomas is a model of moderation. In the *Commentary on the Sentences* he says that the two views of the motive of the Incarnation are equally probable (cf. 4 *Sent*, d.1, q.1, a. 3). In the *Summa Theologiae* he says that it is "more fitting" (*convenientius*) to hold that the Incarnation was ordained by God as a remedy for sin (cf. ST 3a 1, 3).
8. MP p. 154.
9. TD 2/2, p. 233. The purpose of Christ's redemptive work is to enable men to enter into the divine life of the Trinity (cf. TD 3, p. 223).
10. MP p. 133. Balthasar's comments on evolutionary Christologies can be found in C p. 90.

2 The Incarnation, the Cross and the Trinity

[1] TG pp. 27f. On the Trinitarian dimension of the Annunciation, see also VC p. 213; and "Empfangen durch den Heiligen Geist, geboren von der Jungfrau Maria" in W. Sandfachs (ed.), *Ich glaube. Vierzehn Betrachtungen zum apostolischen Glaubensbekenntnis* (Würzburg, 1975), pp. 39–49. Balthasar commends *Lumen Gentium* for casting a Trinitarian light on Mary (ARA, p. 169. Cf. LG pp. 52, 53, 65).

[2] On the appearance of the Trinity in medieval paintings of the Annunciation, see G. Schiller, *Iconography of Christian Art*, vol. 1 (London, 1971), pp. 45f.

[3] St John of the Cross, *Poems*. With a translation by Roy Campbell (London, 1979), p. 75.

[4] Cf. H 3/2/2, pp. 236ff.

[5] TG p. 110. Cf. MP pp. 269ff.

[6] DS p. 426.

[7] ARA p. 115.

[8] Cf. TD 2/2, p. 198.

[9] ARA, pp. 112ff.

[10] See KL passim and Löser, pp. 181–212.

[11] TD pp. 4, 11. Cf. K. Rahner, *Schriften zur Theologie* 15 (1983), pp. 210–213.

[12] On "Inclusion in Christ", see TD 2/2, pp. 211–238.

[13] "The economy (*oikonomia*) is the manifestation of a loving Triune God. So, precisely because only the Son becomes man, Father and Spirit have their own personal part to play in this Incarnation. The part of the Father is his 'good pleasure', the Spirit's his 'cooperation', while it falls to the Son to act in his own person" (KL, 98).

[14] TD 2/2, p. 466.

[15] TD 3, pp. 298f.

[16] Ibid., pp. 297f. Cf. also pp. 273f and TD 4,

pp. 148–155.

[17] Ibid., p. 300.

[18] TD 2/2, p. 466.

[19] TD 3, p. 300.

[20] In the words of the pseudo-Athanasian Creed, ". . . not by the conversion of Godhead into flesh, but by the taking up of manhood into God (. . . *non conversione divinitatis in carnem, sed assumptione humanitatis in Deum)"* (DS 76).

[21] *De recta fide ad Reginas;* PG 76.1205B.

[22] *Epistola ad Epictetum* 6; PG 26.1060C. Cf. TD 4, pp. 195f.

[23] TD 3, pp. 301f.

[24] ST 3a 2, 7. Cf. TD 4, pp. 200f.

[25] TD 2/1, p. 45.

[26] TD 4, p. 200.

[27] Ibid.

[28] TD 3, p. 302.

[29] *Dieu souffre-t-il?* (Paris, 1976), pp. 175f.

[30] TD 4, p. 218.

[31] "Quelques réflexions sur le savoir théologique", *Revue Thomiste* 77 (1969), pp. 5–27; cf. TD 4, pp. 216ff.

[32] "This mysterious perfection which in God is the unnamed exemplar of suffering in us *is an integral part of divine beatitude* – a perfect but exultant peace infinitely above what is humanly conceivable, burning in its flames what for us is apparently irreconcilable: it exults at one and the same time in the eternal splendours of glorious possession, for which (at least for a number of which) we have proper names, and also in the eternal splendour of victorious acceptance, for which we have no proper name, but which, having been made known to us in the image *par excellence*, the image of the flesh and blood of the Son of God suffering death and risen (though keeping for eternity his five hence-

forth glorious wounds), is one day recalled for us, in a kind of living, holy 'metaphor', in the glorious tears of Mary when she moaned and wept before the two little shepherds [at La Salette]'' (Ibid., p. 22).

33 TD 4, p. 221.
34 AC p. 40.
35 TD 3, p. 305.
36 TD 2/1, p. 9.
37 KH 1, p. 232.
38 H 3/2/2, p. 197.
39 For a modern ontology of relation, see the work by the Greek Orthodox theologian, J. Zizioulas, *Being as Communion* (London, 1985).
40 ST 1a 39, 1.
41 *Expositio super Dionysium de divinis nominibus* 5, lect. 3. Cf. M. J. Woods, *The Unchanging God of Love*. A Study of the Teaching of St Thomas Aquinas on Divine Immutability in View of Certain Contemporary Criticism of this Doctrine (Fribourg, 1986), pp. 214f.
42 Woods, pp. 217f.
43 Ibid., p. 227.
44 Woods, pp. 229ff.

3 Christ and Analogy

1 TD 2/2, pp. 202–210; TD 4, pp. 353–355; TL 2, pp. 284–288; Marchesi, pp. 348ff.
2 Cf. TD 1, passim; UA p. 92f.
3 TD 2/2, p. 140.
4 TD 1, pp. 605f.
5 ST 1a 43, 2, ad 3.
6 TD 2/2, pp. 152f.
7 TD 2/2, p. 157.
8 TD 2/2, pp. 151ff, 472ff.

9 TD 1, p. 606.
10 Cf. TD 2/1, p. 31.
11 TD 3, p. 51.
12 TG p. 30.
13 TD 4, p. 224, quoting Adrienne.
14 CS pp. 78f.
15 "We must get away from a subordinationist or
Arian view of the redemption: a supreme God the
Father issuing orders to an inferior God (*deuteros
theos*) or demigod or superman. No, as Christians
our starting-point can only be a consubstantial
(*homoousios*) Trinity, in which the freedom, dignity
and spontaneity of the Son and Spirit are as divine
as the Father's, a Trinity in which the Son and Spirit
do not just approve and execute the orders of the
Father's creative and salvific plan, but conceive it at
the very beginning in the most perfect unity with
him. Now, in this plan of salvation, it is the Son
who will have to suffer in order to justify this
world, even though guilty, being judged finally as
'very good'; it is he who will have to bear its weight
like a spiritual Atlas. So it is not enough to think of
him just acquiescing in what the Father proposes.
No, we have to accept that the proposal proceeds
originally from him, that he offers himself to the
Father in order to sustain and save the work of
creation. And it seems to me that this proposal of
the Son's touches the heart of the Father – to speak
in human terms – more profoundly than even the
world's sin; it opens in God a wound of love from
before the creation – or, if you like, it is the sign and
expression of this ever-open wound in the heart of
the Trinity, a wound identical with the procession
and circumincession of the divine persons in their
perfect beatitude. This wound comes before the
one St Anselm is concerned with, namely, the
offence done to the Father by sin, the offence

expiated by the Son, the only one capable of this work, which must be supererogatory. And if the wound of which we speak comes before all this, there is no problem in accepting that, for the salvation of the world, the Father sends the Son, guided on earth by the Spirit, who at every moment indicates to him the will of the Father, and that this will is at once an infinite love of creatures and infinite respect for the offer of the Son, which has been accepted by the Father and allowed by the Spirit to be realized, to the point of that supreme diastasis of the Father and Son on the Cross, which is in truth the ultimate revelation of the tripersonality of God" (AC pp. 39f).

16 CS pp. 78f.
17 TD 2/1, p. 242. On the significance of the term *tropos* in the Triadology and Christology of St Maximus, see J.-M. Garrigues, *Maxime le Confesseur. La charité, avenir divin de l'homme* (Paris, 1976), pp. 106f.
18 FG p. 59.
19 TL 3, p. 180.
20 TL 3, p. 22.
21 On "Trinitarian inversion", see TD 2/2, pp. 167–175.
22 TD 3, p. 158. "The fact that Jesus truly possesses the Spirit 'without measure' within himself and yet acknowledges [the Spirit] to be 'above him' is the expression of his self-abasement (*status exinanitionis*) . . . But this Spirit of God who is above him, whom he obeys as the expression of the Father's will, in whom, at every stage, he perceives the concrete form his mission must take, this Spirit who 'drives' him (Mt.12:28) is at the same time *in* him, as we see, for example, when he 'drives out evil spirits in the Spirit of God' (Mt.12:28). This Spirit, both in and above him, is, therefore, the

manifest presence of his divine mission" (TD 2/2,
p. 477).

23 TD 2/2, p. 477.
24 Cf. St Cyril's ninth anathematism (DS 260).
25 TD 2/2, p. 477.
26 TL 3, pp. 157f.
27 *In Epistolas Omnes D. Pauli*, tom. 7 (Venice, 1600),
 p. 259.
28 TD 2/2, p. 478; TL 2, p. 142; TL pp. 3, 167.
29 TL 3, p. 160.
30 TD 2/2, p. 478.
31 GIRM 55 (f).
32 H 3/1, p. 466.
33 AH 1, p. 12.
34 For the role of Ignatius in the collaborative mission
 of Adrienne and Balthasar, see Adrienne's *Igna-
 tiana*, new ed. (Einsiedeln, 1985).
35 MP p. 147.
36 MP p. 147.
37 MP p. 153. Balthasar makes a carefully discriminat-
 ing use of Bulgakov. He keeps clear of the "sophi-
 ology", but builds on the Russian's insights into
 the unselfishness (*désintéressement*) of the divine
 persons as pure relations within the intradivine life
 of love. "This *désintéressement* is the basis of a
 primary form of kenosis, which is realized in creation (above all, of free man), since the Creator, so
 to speak, yields part of his freedom to the creature,
 but ultimately he only risks this adventure in virtue
 of the foreknowledge and acceptance of the second
 kenosis in the proper sense of the word, the
 kenosis of the Cross, in which the Creator meets
 and overcomes the most extreme consequences of
 created liberty. In this way the kenosis – as the
 abandonment of the 'form of God' – becomes
 without doubt the distinctive act of the love of the
 Son, who makes his generation (and thus his

dependence on the Father) take the expressive form of created obedience. Nevertheless, the whole Trinity is involved in this act: the Father is the one who sends the Son and abandons him on the Cross; the Spirit who no longer unifies the two persons except in the form of separation (H 3/2/2, p. 198, citing Bulgakov, *Du Verbe incarné: Agnus Dei* (Paris, 1943), passim).

"The Father, who begets the Son, does not 'lose' himself in that act to Another in order only thus to 'attain' himself; it is precisely as the One who gives himself that he *always* is himself. And the Son, too, is always himself by letting himself be begotten and letting the Father have him at his disposal. The Spirit is always himself by seeing his 'I' as the 'We' of Father and Son, making this expropriation his *propriissimum*. (It is only when we understand this that we escape from the machinery of Hegel's dialectic)" (TD 2/1, p. 232).

[38] MP p. 148.

[39] Cf. TD 3, p. 301.

[40] Ibid.

[41] Ibid.

[42] TD 2/1, p. 233.

[43] TD 3, p. 303.

[44] TD 2/1, p. 232.

[45] MP p. 147.

[46] Ibid.

[47] MP p. 153.

[48] DS 3002.

[49] DS 3025.

[50] ST 1a 44, 4, ad 1.

[51] TD 2/2, p. 264.

[52] According to St Thomas, the revelation of the Trinity was necessary for a right understanding of the freedom with which God created the world: "By maintaining that God made everything

162

through his Word, we avoid the error of those who hold that God's nature compelled him to create things. By affirming that there is in him the procession of love, we show that he made creatures, not because he needed them, nor because of any reason outside of himself, but from love of his own goodness" (1a 32, 1, ad 3).

53 TD 2/1, pp. 186–258.

54 TL 2, pp. 171–174.

55 TD 3, p. 301. "The act by which the Father expresses and gives the whole of his divinity (an act which he not only 'does' but 'is'), inasmuch as it generates the Son as the One who is infinitely Other to himself, must be at the same time the eternal presupposition and overcoming of all that separation, pain, estrangement will be in the world, and what loving devotion, the opportunity for encounter, happiness mean there too. Not direct identity of the two, but superior and surpassing presupposition for both" (TD 3, p. 302).

"The fact that God (as Father) can give away his divinity in such a way that God (as Son) not only receives it as lent but possesses it 'consubstantially' implies such an incomprehensible and unsurpassable 'separation' of God from himself that any separation made possible (by it!), even the darkest and most bitter, can only take place within it" (TD 3, p. 302).

56 TD 3, p. 308.

57 H 3/2/2, p. 200.

58 MP pp. 151f.

59 *Oratio catechetica* 24; PG 45.64CD.

60 TL 2, pp. 13ff; TL 3, pp. 57–94; "Gott ist sein eigener Exeget", IKZ (1986), pp. 8–13.

61 H 3/2/2; p. 131

62 Cf. CM pp. 61f; Adrienne, WP pp. 103ff.

63 CM p. 38.

[64] Ibid.

[65] H 3/2/2, pp. 69ff.

[66] Eph.19, 1; ed. J.B. Lightfoot, *The Apostolic Fathers. Revised Texts* (London, 1907), p. 105.

[67] *Epistola ad Magnesios* 8, 2; ed. Lightfoot, p. 114.

[68] CM p. 39.

[69] *Much Ado About Nothing*, Act 2, Scene 1.

[70] IKZ (1986), 11.

[71] *De contemplando Deo* 10; SC 61, pp. 92f.

[72] TL 3, pp. 61ff; TL 2, pp. 14ff.

[73] IKZ (1986), p. 12.

[74] TL 3, p. 14.

[75] TL 3, p. 27.

[76] *Adversus Haereses* 3, 24, 1; SC 211, p. 474. Cf. TL 3, p. 15.

4 Incarnate and Crucified for Us

[1] TG p. 91; cf. AC p. 11.

[2] TD 2/2, pp. 218–225.

[3] *Des heiligen Ephraem des Syrers Paschahymnen*, tr. E. Beck (Louvain, 1964), p. 3.

[4] SP p. 86.

[5] "He aligns four concepts, all of which perceive one aspect of the mystery, but all, too, need to be surpassed. All are mutually complementary, each indispensable, each on its own insufficient: merit, satisfaction, sacrifice, redemption (or ransom)" (AC p. 65).

[6] Cf. TD 3, pp. 221–223.

[7] DK p. 76.

[8] MP pp. 224f; cf. also pp. 405–407.

[9] AC p. 25.

[10] Cf. TD 3, p. 327.

[11] TD 3, pp. 222, 363.

[12] AC p. 23.

[13] AC p. 75.

[14] TD 3, p. 313.

[15] DK pp. 75f.

[16] ST 3a 46, 6.

[17] AC pp. 36f.

[18] TG p. 71. The quotation from George Herbert comes from his poem "The Agonie" (*The Works of George Herbert*, ed. F.E. Hutchinson (Oxford, 1941), p. 37).

[19] TG p. 79.

[20] KH 1, p. 255.

[21] KH 2, p. 213.

[22] UA, p. 54.

[23] TD 3, p. 311.

[24] "In this darkness and the alienation it involves between God and the Son bearing the sins of men, the love of God, in both its almightiness and its unmightiness, shines out: the Son must identify himself with the darkness for substitution to be possible" (Bätzing, p. 46; TD 3, p. 312).

[25] See the comments of the Orthodox writer, Olivier Clément, *Questions sur l'homme* (Paris, 1972), pp. 47f.

[26] AC p. 25.

[27] "On the Cross Christ confesses to the Father the sin of the whole of humanity: the monstrous reality of the world's sin, already committed and still to be committed, with its dreadful, grotesque face, which he can no longer endure and on whose account he dies in the nakedness and uselessness of the Cross" (KH 1, p. 365).

[28] Conf, p. 21.

[29] Ibid., p. 23.

[30] KH 1, p. 170.

[31] H 3/2/2, p. 193.

[32] DS 1331.

[33] TD 3, p. 306.

[34] MP p. 200.

35 TD 3, p. 221.
36 H 3/2/2, p. 208. On the wrath of God, see also TD 3, pp. 52f, 315f; AC pp. 22f.
37 UA p. 54.
38 H 3/2/2, pp. 195f.
39 TD 3, p. 310.
40 Ep.96. The next quotation in the text is from DK 75.
41 TD 4, p. 236.
42 OR (1988), n. 49, p. 1.
43 ST 3a 50, 2, ad 1.
44 OR (1988), n. 49, p. 15.
45 ST 3a 15, 10.
46 ST 3a 9, and q.10.
47 ST 3a 46, 6.
48 OR (1988), n. 49, p. 1. For a defence and re-statement of the traditional Scholastic doctrine of a threefold human knowledge in Christ, see B. de Margerie SJ, *The Human Knowledge of Christ: The Knowledge, Foreknowledge and Consciousness, Even in the Pre-Paschal Period, of Christ the Redeemer*, ET (Boston, 1980. On the point in question, see pp. 40ff).
49 "Ist der Gekreuzigte selig?", IKZ (1987), p. 108. Cf. his comments in TL: "The idea of Jesus enjoying the beatific vision of God at the "summit" of his soul, while the "lower parts of the soul" experience Godforsakenness, nowadays seems quite incredible and cannot be salvaged by the arguments adduced" (TL 261n).
50 TL 2, pp. 261ff.
51 Cf. ST 3a 46, 8.
52 "At the moment of his death he was certainly annihilated in his soul, without any consolation or relief, since the Father left him that way in inner-most aridity in the lower part. He was thereby compelled to cry out: 'My God, my God, why have you forsaken me?' This was the most extreme

abandonment, sensitively, that he had suffered in his life" (*The Ascent of Mount Carmel* 2, 7, 11; *The Collected Works of St John of the Cross*, ET (Washington, 1979), p. 124).

53 Cf. J. Maritain, *On the Grace and Humanity of Jesus*, ET (London, 1969), pp. 48ff.

54 But see Balthasar's criticisms of Albert Frank-Duquesne's attempt to harmonize joy and Godforsakenness in the Passion in WS, pp. 133ff. See also Löser, pp. 243f.

55 Louis Chardon OP, *La Croix de Jésus*. New ed. (Paris, 1937), pp. 48f and passim.

5 *Mary and the Mysteries of March*

1 ARA p. 116.

2 EH 1, 271. On the interrelation of Trinitarian doctrine, Christology, and Mariology, see E p. 66.

3 ARA p. 115.

4 AC p. 54.

5 E 72.

6 ARA p. 164.

7 LG 56.

8 St Augustine, *Sermo* 215, 4; PL 38.1074; St Leo the Great, *In Nativitate Domini* 1, 1; SC 22B, p. 68. Cf. RM 13. 9; AC pp. 55f.

9 AC p. 55f.

10 TD 2/2, p. 273.

11 For example, Julian of Norwich refers to Our Lord's "courtayse love" (*A Book of Showings to the Anchoress Julian of Norwich*, ed. E. Colledge and J. Walsh, part 1 (Toronto, 1978), p. 211).

12 LG 56.

13 FG p. 51.

14 WP pp. 97–125; CM pp. 53–66.

15 "Mary's being towards her Child (*Das Hin-Sein*

Marias zum Kind) is essentially prayer" (CM p. 60).

[16] Cf. TD 3, pp. 333f; TdG pp. 162–188.

[17] GL 1, p. 564.

[18] MPE p. 8.

[19] TD 3, pp. 329f.

[20] ST 3a 30, 1; cf. C. Feckes (ed.), *Die heilsgeschichtliche Stellvertretung der Menschheit durch Maria* (Paderborn, 1954), passim.

[21] SV 171.

[22] TD 2/2, pp. 261f.

[23] TD 2/2, p. 264. Again developing an insight of Adrienne's, Balthasar acknowledges that there is a certain analogical femininity about the Son's relation to the Father, his eternal receiving of the divine essence from the Father. Since the eternal, uncreated Son is the archetype of all that is created in time, he is archetypal of both masculine and feminine – of the feminine by his passive receptivity towards the Father, of the masculine by his active gratitude for what he receives. However, when he becomes man, he becomes male, "because, as the One sent by the Father, he represents the Father's authority within creation. With regard to creation and the Church, he is under no circumstances primarily the receiver but the producer (*der Hervorbringende*)" ("Die Würde der Frau", (*Homo Creatus Est*. Skizzen zur Theologie V (Einsiedeln, 1986), p. 140)). Neither Father nor Son can be anything other than analogically male with regard to the creature. For Adrienne's insights, see EH 3, 2039 and 2255.

[24] AC p. 58.

[25] See M. Hauke, *Women in the Priesthood*. A Systematic Analysis in the Light of the Order of Creation and Redemption (San Francisco, 1988), pp. 304f.

[26] FG p. 51.

[27] MPE p. 49.
[28] LB pp. 40f.
[29] FG p. 81.
[30] ARA p. 172.
[31] Gerard Manley Hopkins, "The Blessed Virgin compared to the Air we Breathe", *Poems*, 3rd ed. (London, New York & Toronto, 1948), p. 100.
[32] HL p. 9.
[33] See pp. 26–27 above.
[34] EH 3, 2109. "Mary's word of assent can be a participation in the quality of the son's consent. This quality can only be bestowed on her in advance by God, not as something alien but as the capability for the deepest self-realization. For God is eternal freedom, and, in giving himself, he can only free the creature to highest freedom" (TG p. 32).
[35] ARA p. 172.
[36] FG p. 51.
[37] MH pp. 16f.
[38] Ibid., 15; cf. St Thérèse of Lisieux. *Poésies*. Un cantique d'amour (Paris, 1979), pp. 242–248; Pope John Paul II, RM 17.
[39] AC p. 66; HL p. 111.
[40] AC pp. 65f.
[41] Ibid., pp. 66f.
[42] AC pp. 66f.
[43] HL p. 111.
[44] ARA p. 172.
[45] TD 3, p. 369.
[46] TD 3, pp. 376f.
[47] ARA p. 164.
[48] ARA p. 150.
[49] ME pp. 42f.
[50] AC pp. 62f.
[51] AC p. 13.
[52] AC p. 54. Jesus' relation to Mary as a woman has

both individual and social aspects (TD 2/2, p. 265). Balthasar does not speak, as Scheeben did, of Our Lady's "spousal motherhood" (cf. his *Handbuch der katholischen Dogmatik*, Band III (Freiburg, 1933), p. 491f.).

[53] TD 3, pp. 327f.

[54] MH p. 13.

[55] ARA p. 143.

[56] UA p. 105.

[57] ARA p. 116.

[58] ARA p. 189.

[59] TG p. 103.

[60] Ibid.

[61] UA p. 56.

[62] Ibid., pp. 105f.

[63] Cf. ARA p. 187.

[64] UA pp. 105f.

[65] UA p. 106.

[66] "Epilog: Die marianische Prägung der Kirche" in W. Beinert (ed.), *Maria heute ehren*, 2nd ed. (Freiburg etc., 1977), p. 276.

[67] HL p. 133.

[68] TD 3, pp. 371, 377.

[69] MPE p. 59. In 1977, in his official capacity as a member of the International Theological Commission, Balthasar wrote an important article in *L'Osservatore Romano* expounding the Sacred Congregation for the Doctrine of the Faith's document *Inter Insigniores* on the ordination of women. Balthasar describes the Church's teaching on this subject as an "uninterrupted tradition", which is not "a kind of archaism" but derives from the Church's "faithfulness to her Founder" (*L'Osservatore Romano* (1977), n. 8, p. 6). The order of redemption perfects, does not destroy, the order of creation, so "the redemptive mystery 'Christ-Church' is the superabundant fulfilment of the

mystery of the creation of man and woman". The maleness of the priesthood derives from and expresses this nuptial mystery: only males can represent the male Christ. Developing some insights of Louis Bouyer, Balthasar points out that representation is a typically masculine function, but it is a sign of a kind of poverty within the male: as a sexual being, he "represents what he is not and transmits what he does not actually possess", whereas "woman rests on herself, she is fully what she is, that is, the whole reality of a created being that faces God as a partner" (ibid.). Male ministerial representation is "secondary and instrumental", but femininity is the Church's truest identity. The weak and sinful males who exercise the ordained ministry remedy their deficiencies precisely by participating more deeply in the "comprehensive femininity of the Marian Church . . . by learning to express and live better the *fiat* that Mary addressed to God One and Triune" (ibid.). He concludes: "It should give woman a feeling of exaltation to know that she – particularly in the Virgin Mother Mary – is the privileged place where God can and wishes to be received in the world" (ibid., p. 7). M. Hauke (see n. 25) has developed the ideas of Balthasar in his masterly defence of the necessary maleness of the ministerial priesthood.

6 *The Mass and the Mysteries of March*

1 The whole Gospel, according to Adrienne, is bracketed by the Incarnation and the Eucharist (cf. OM p. 529).
2 ME pp. 60f.
3 EH 1, 266.
4 MH p. 39. In EH Balthasar records the following

conversation with Adrienne. "At my communion she saw how Mary received Communion beside me and, as it were, in me. This was something quite new for her. Mary received the Lord in everyone who communicates and receives perfectly, while the communicant receives him only, as it were, incompletely. But the Mother receives him on the communicant's behalf and in order to mediate to him the grace of communion, so that, so to speak, nothing is lost from that grace. She, as it were, stores up the grace for the person concerned in order to supply him with it when he needs it. Suppose a person, at the time he receives Holy Communion, is without sin, but then an hour later commits a venial sin (e.g. by a harsh word). Then again, an hour later, in his dealings with other people, he needs total purity anew: at that moment Mary will mediate to him the grace of his morning's communion again. It's like a little child in the arms of his mother being given an orange by someone. The mother gives it to the child to hold but then ensures that the child doesn't drop it. In the end she will eat the orange herself, because the child is too young to, and yet she eats it, if you like, for the child. ('At this point', says A., 'the example begins to break down')" (EH 1, 608).

5 TG p. 38.
6 NE p. 113; H 3/2/2, p. 137.
7 MP p. 192.
8 NE p. 115.
9 MP p. 191.
10 DS 1740–1741.
11 DS 1743.
12 *De Civitate Dei* 10, 20; PL 41.298.
13 DS 1741.
14 SP pp. 95f.
15 SC 208.

16 AC pp. 52f.

17 TD 3, p. 378.

18 *Marie, L'Église et le sacerdoce*, 2 vols. (Paris, 1952–1953).

19 TD 3, pp. 332–334.

20 TD 3, p. 372.

21 TD 3, p. 377.

22 M.J. Scheeben, *Handbuch der katholischen Dogmatik*, vol. 2 (Freiburg, 1933), p. 922.

23 SP, pp. 93f.

24 TD 3, pp. 301, 303.

25 NE p. 115.

26 TD 3, p. 221.

27 E pp. 120f.

28 *The Way of Perfection*, ch. 33 in *The Complete Works of St Teresa of Jesus*, vol. ii, tr. and ed. E. Allison Peers (London, 1946), p. 143.

29 NE p. 117.

30 NE p. 120.

31 NE pp. 118f.

32 PI p. 25.

33 Cited in the preface to Bernanos' *Oeuvres romanesques* (Paris, 1961), p. liv.

7 *Lady Day, Good Friday, All Saints' Day*

1 TD 3, p. 379.

2 Ibid., p. 380.

3 TD 2/1, p. 46.

4 *Le Désespéré*, new ed. (Paris, 1964), p. 113.

5 See EH passim.

6 FG p. 74.

7 E p. 62.

8 WP pp. 25f.

9 EH 3, 2283.

[10] *Catholicisme*. Les aspects sociaux du dogme (Paris, 1938).

[11] EH 1, 11.

[12] See the paper by an anonymous Jesuit, "Arm um zu bereichern" in Symp, 36.

[13] EH 1, 93f.

[14] EH 1, 341.

[15] Cf. H 3/2/2, pp. 430f.

[16] TD 3, p. 381.

[17] *Homiliae in Leviticum* 4, 4; cf. TD 3, p. 381.

[18] *Sermo* 71, 20; cited, ibid.

[19] H 3/2/2, p. 436.

[20] Cf. DS 1691.

[21] TD 3, p. 383.

[22] *In Symb.*, art. 10.

[23] TD 3, pp. 393f.

[24] When the convent is looted, the Prioress says: "However poor we may be henceforth, we shall only be imitating our Master from afar. We are still not as poor as Him" (Act 4, Scene 3).

[25] Cf. TD 3, pp. 393f. See also Balthasar's *Le chrétien Bernanos* (Paris, 1956), passim, and "Georges Bernanos: Hölle und Freude" in SC, pp. 407–414.

8 Lady Day and Holy Saturday

[1] *The Harp of the Spirit*. Eighteen Poems of Saint Ephrem. Introduction and translation by S. Brock (London, 1983), p. 27.

[2] Cf. MP p. 145. On the theme of descent in Balthasar's Christology, see Marchesi, pp. 151ff.

[3] DS 294.

[4] Cf. St Thomas Aquinas, *In Jo*, cap. 3, lect. 2.

[5] MP p. 228.

[6] Ibid.

[7] Cf. St Bonaventure, *Dominica XII post Pentecosten, Sermo 1*; Quaracchi ed., t. 9, 398f.

[8] *Adversus Haereses* 3, 20, 3; SC 211, p. 392.

[9] VC pp. 186f.

[10] On Balthasar's critique of "Prometheanism", see Marchesi pp. 4f, 41ff.

[11] The atheistic glorification of abstract Man leads to the destruction of concrete men. The idealized humanity of the godless humanisms turns out to be the select few (the Party, the Master Race, the Working Class), to whose interests all others can be sacrificed. In Hegel, Balthasar says, the human individual is "sacrificed to the realized idea"; in Marx to "the idea to be realized" (C pp. 55f). Of Hegel he says: "When . . . the divine becomes the 'universal' (with nothing more exalted above it), the individual as individual, already subordinated in favour of Spirit's self-consciousness, is eliminated in favour of the whole as well: physically through death, and aesthetically by giving itself up to the whole" (H 3/1/2, p. 920).

Balthasar's mentor, Henri Cardinal de Lubac, has shown how all the modern atheistic ideologies, however great the contrast between them, have a common foundation – the rejection of God – and "a certain similarity in results, the chief of which is the annihilation of the human person" (de Lubac, *The Drama of Atheistic Humanism*, ET (London, 1949). Nietzsche and Wagner are not Hitler, Marx and Engels are not Stalin, and yet the later "distortions are often not so much betrayals as the effects of an inevitable corruption". "Atheist humanism was bound to end in bankruptcy. Man is himself only because his face is illumined by a divine ray . . . If the fire disappears, the reflected gleam immediately dies out" (de Lubac, 31f.) Man is great only because God is greater. He cannot deify himself.

He can only receive divinization as a grace from the God who humbled himself to assume the condition of a slave.

12 *The Lenten Triodion*, ET (London & Boston, 1978), p. 625.

13 Maas p. 245. On Balthasar's theology of the Descent in relation to his interpretation of the Fathers, see Löser, pp. 237–246.

14 UA pp. 81f.

15 KH 1, p. 11.

16 Ibid., p. 10.

17 KH 1, p. 275.

18 On the Descent into Hell in the Apostles' Creed, see J.N.D. Kelly, *Early Christian Creeds* 3rd ed. (London, 1973), pp. 378f.

19 The Descent into Hell emerges as a theological issue during the Apollinarian controversy. According to Apollinarius, the Logos did not assume a complete human nature; he himself took the place of the rational spiritual soul (*nous*) and performed all the functions normally exercised by it. Against this view, the Fathers say that it means that Christ's death on the Cross is not a real human death at all, for there is no separation of soul and body, but only the separation of divinity and flesh. As Grillmeier says, "you cannot talk about Christ's Descent if you deny he had a soul. The Logos alone, the omni-present God, is not capable of descent into or ascent out of the underworld. Only the soul of Christ can do that" ("Der Gottessohn im Toten-reich. Soteriologische und christologische Moti-vierung der Descensuslehre in der älteren christli-chen Überlieferung", in *Mit ihm und in ihm: Christologische Forschungen und Perspektiven* (Frei-burg, Basel and Wien, 1975), p. 131).

In one of the anti-Apollinarian treatises attri-buted to St Athanasius, we find the following:

"The loud cry and the manifestation of the soul do not announce the separation of the divinity but signify the death of the body. Thereby the divinity does not abandon the body lying in the grave, nor is it separated from the soul in Hades" (2, 14; PG 26. 1154BC).

"Death and the departure of the spirit (*pneuma*) did not mean the departure of God from the body, but the separation of the soul from the body" (2, 15; PG 26. 1157A).

To understand St Athanasius' argument we must remember his strong sense of the inclusiveness of Christ's humanity. The fact that the possessor of that humanity is the Logos, the Creator of the universe, means that his human actions and sufferings have a universal efficacy and scope. This human death is the death not of a mere man but of him through whom all things were made, the Head of the Body, the first-born from the dead (2, 15; 1157C). The incarnate Word truly dies *our* human death, which means that his saving death touches the death of every man. If Apollinarius were right, this would not happen; he would have died some private death of his own, unrelated to human mortality. "If death and the demise of the body took place by the removal (*metastasis*) of the Godhead, then he dies his own death and not ours" (1, 18; 1125B).

A "divine death", were such an absurdity possible, would have no saving significance for us; our human death would be untouched by it (see G.D. Dragas, *St Athanasius: Contra Apollinarem* (Athens, 1985), pp. 224–288).

[20] Cf. *Epistola ad Magnesios* 9, 2; Lightfoot, 114. Maas argues that the background to Matt. 27 is Ezek. 37:12. In the Dura-Europos synagogue there are pictures that appear to represent some kind of

descent by the Messiah. The Jews seem to have speculated about a *descensus ad inferos* by the Messiah (Maas p. 97).

21 Maas, pp. 67ff.

22 "We cannot trace Christ's story between the moment of his death and 'the first day of the week . . . early, while it was yet dark'. This passage indicates that that interval was not without significance, and that in it, as at other times, Jesus Christ was active as the Saviour of the world. The best thing is to realize that we encounter here a mystery, which is still a secret from us, and reverently to accept the hint that is given to us. It is a hint within the canon of Scripture that the atoning efficacy of Christ's death was available to those who died in paganism in the ages before Christ, and also, surely, a hint that those who in subsequent ages have died without ever having had a real chance to believe in him are not beyond the reach of his saving power" (*I and II Peter and Jude: Introduction and Commentary* (London, 1960), p. 103f.).

23 Cf. Maas, pp. 109ff.

24 Cf. ST 3a 49, 5; 52, 5.

25 KH 2, pp. 90–92; TL 2, p. 337.

26 KH 1, p. 79.

27 Cf. ST 3a 52, 3.

28 *Homilia in Sabbatum Sanctum* 2; PG 96, 601D–604A.

29 3 *Sent.* d. 2, q. 2, a. 1.

30 Cf. a sermon of St Germanus of Constantinople: "'Adam, where are you?' He asks again. 'I have come to search for you, and to find you.'" (*Oratio in Dominici Corporis Sepulturam*; PG 98.257C).

31 ST 3a 50, 4.

32 MP p. 248.

33 Cf. KH 2, pp. 208, 337.

34 Cf. KH 1, p. 56.

35 MP p. 248.
36 Cf. MP p. 72.
37 MP p. 248.
38 MP pp. 246–248.
39 MP p. 248.
40 Cf. KH 2, pp. 20, 27.
41 MP p. 238.
42 Ibid., p. 234.
43 *Oratio in Dominici Corporis Sepulturam*; PG 98.257C.
44 KH 1, p. 65.
45 KH 1, p. 63.
46 "Since the Father must be considered as the Creator of human freedom (with all its foreseen consequences!), judgement and thus Hell also belong to him as his original possession. When he sends the Son into the world to save it instead of judging it, and when for this role of Saviour he 'gives all judgement to the Son' (Jn.5.22), he must also introduce the Son *made man* into Hell, which is the supreme consequence of human freedom. But the Son can only be introduced into Hell as dead, on Holy Saturday. This introduction is necessary since the dead 'must hear the voice of the Son of God' and, hearing it, 'live' (Jn.5.25)" (MP p. 248).

"[Hell] is in fact a mystery of the Father as creator, an ultimate consequence of that divine love in which he created human beings for freedom and so had given the possibility of saying not only Yes but No to him" (Maas, Symp, 134. Cf. KH 1, p. 106).

47 The phrase "lumber room" comes from Mgr Ronald Knox's exposition of the Descent into Hell in *The Creed in Slow Motion* (London, 1949), pp. 110f.
48 KH 1, pp. 175, 244.
49 AH 1, p. 22.
50 JK 4, p. 174.

51 Cf. KH 1, p. 265.

52 KH 1, p. 107.

53 Cf. ST 1a 37, 2, ad 3.

54 KH 1, pp. 190f.

55 ST 3a 52, 2.

56 MP p. 246.

57 FG p. 66.

58 MP p. 171.

59 Cf. MP p. 167.

60 *Was dürfen wir hoffen?* (Einsiedeln, 1986), passim.

61 MP p. 249.

62 OM p. 295; C p. 55; KH 1, p. 172. "The sins he meets in Hell are sins without sinners" (KH 1, p. 172).

63 UA pp. 54f.

64 KH 1, p. 111.

65 Balthasar, Symp p. 143; cf. KH 1, p. 227.

66 *Adversus Haereses* 4, 22, 1; SC 100/2, p. 688.

67 Alexander of Hales, *Summa Theologica* 3, tr. 7, q. 1, a. 1; Quaracchi ed. t. 4, n. 205, p. 291.

68 *Excitationes*, lib. 10 (Basel, 1565), p. 659.

69 TL 2, p. 320.

70 ST 3a 52, 1.

71 *Moralia* 10, 9; PL 75.929A.

72 MP p. 246.

73 *The Lenten Triodion*, pp. 622, 628.

74 MP p. 248.

75 MP p. 251. Cf. TD 4, pp. 329–337.

76 Balthasar, Symp 141.

77 OM p. 356.

78 *Ennarrationes in Psalmes* 30, 8; PL 36.252.

79 SV p. 282.

80 *In symb.*, art. 10.

81 LG 62.

82 Cf. TL 2, pp. 326f.

83 See the comments above about Bernanos' *Carmelites* (pp. 100f.).

84 TL 2, p. 327.
85 *The Ascent of Mount Carmel* 2, 7, 11; ET, p. 125.
86 *The Dark Night of the Soul* 2, 6, 6; ET, p. 339f.
87 On the night of St John of the Cross and the Descent into Hell, see KH 1, pp. 210, 241, and 265. St Teresa's account of her mystical experiences in Hell can be found in her *Life*, ET, J.M. Cohen (Harmondsworth, 1957), pp. 233ff. On Staretz Silouan, see Archimandrite Sophrony, *The Monk of Mount Athos: Staretz Silouan 1866–1938*, ET (London and Oxford, 1973), pp. 115ff.
88 Symp p. 143.
89 Symp pp. 146f. The next quotation in the text comes from Symp p. 146.
90 TD 2/2, p. 456. Cf. *Was dürfen wir hoffen?* (Einsiedeln, 1986), p. 118; J. Ratzinger "Abschied vom Teufel" in *Dogma und Verkündigung* (Munich and Freiburg, 1973), p. 233).
91 Maas, Symp p. 128f.
92 Balthasar, Symp p. 144.

Glorious Mysteries

1 Cf. MP p. 256.
2 TG p. 110.
3 On "the Crucified as the Risen One" see TD 3, pp. 337–342; MP pp. 171ff, 182, 212, 271f, 274f, 281ff, 308ff; C pp. 39f; H 3/2/2, pp. 221ff, 296–300, 301–307, 467.
4 GL 1, p. 314.
5 H 3/2/2, p. 340.
6 In 1 Cor. 15; cf. ST 1a 75, 4.
7 ST 1a 75, 4, ad 2. As Balthasar says in his exposition of the eleventh article of the Apostles' Creed, "a fleshless soul is not a man, and reincarnation could

never redeem us from the dilapidation of death''
(Credo, p. 82).

[8] 3a 50, 4.
[9] ST 3a 52, 3.
[10] "Swper yr Arglwydd" by D. Gwenallt Jones in *Poetry of Wales 1930–1970*, ed. R. Gerallt Jones (Gomer Press, Llandysul, 1974), p. 112f.
[11] Cf. MP pp. 257, 260.
[12] DK p. 84.
[13] MP p. 265.
[14] *Epistola ad Smyrnaeos* 3, 1–3; Lightfoot, p. 128.
[15] MP p. 257.
[16] TG pp. 109f; cf. MP pp. 257, 269–281.
[17] MP pp. 272f.
[18] MP p. 270.
[19] Cf. MP p. 270.
[20] Credo, p. 51.
[21] MP p. 273.
[22] MP p. 276.
[23] TG pp. 111f.
[24] MP p. 279.
[25] TG p. 112.
[26] Cf. TH p. 112.
[27] TG p. 113.
[28] TD 3, pp. 341f.
[29] TH p. 114.
[30] Ibid., p. 81.
[31] *Epistola ad Smyrnaeos* 3; Lightfoot, p. 28.
[32] TH p. 82.
[33] TH p. 91.
[34] JK 4, p. 218.
[35] JK 4, pp. 420ff; cf. MP pp. 311ff.
[36] TD 3, p. 338. See also Credo, pp. 84f.
[37] See the SCDF document "The Reality of Life After Death" (11 May 1979) in *Vatican Council II: More Post-Conciliar Documents*, ed. A. Flannery (Leominster, 1982), pp. 501f.

[38] Cf. TD 4, p. 323.
[39] DK p. 170.
[40] Cf. HL p. 146.
[41] DK p. 169.
[42] *Poems of Gerard Manley Hopkins*, 3rd ed. (London, New York, and Toronto, 1948), p. 112.

GLOSSARY

Christology

That part of theology which relates to Christ.

Economy
(Greek, *oikonomia*)

Management, organization, ordering, dispensation, hence the divine dispensation in creation and redemption, "the economy of salvation". For many of the Fathers, from St Justin Martyr (c.100–c.165) onwards, it is virtually a synonym of the Incarnation.

Economic Trinity

The Blessed Trinity revealed in the *economy* of salvation, i.e. in and by the incarnate Son.

Gestalt
(German)

Form, figure (the central concept in Balthasar's *Theological Aesthetic*).

Hypostasis
(Greek)

Literally, something placed under, that which underlies or gives support, now used in theology to mean subsisting subject, person.

Hypostatic union

The union of the divine and human natures in the hypostasis (person) of the divine Word.

Immanent Trinity The eternal, inner life of the Blessed Trinity.

Immutability Unchangeableness, unalterableness.

Impassibility Incapacity for suffering.

Kenosis
(Greek)
Literally, emptying. With reference to Phil. 2.7 ("He emptied himself", *heauton ekenôse*, it means the self-emptying of the Son of God in the Incarnation.

Patripassianism The heresy which attributes suffering to God the Father.

Pneumatology That part of theology which relates to the Holy Spirit.

Promethean Of, pertaining to, or resembling the demi-god Prometheus in Greek mythology, who made man out of clay, stole fire from Olympus, and taught men the use of it. Balthasar uses the term to describe a certain tendency within German Idealism (see p. 107).

Soteriology That part of theology which relates to salvation.

Status exinanitionis
(Latin)
The state of self-emptying, the state in which the incarnate Word lived from his Virginal

185

	Conception to his death on the Cross.
Univocal	Having only one meaning; of the same name and of the same nature.
Via Eminentiae (Latin)	The way of excellence. The method by which something is affirmed of a thing in the form of an endless increase. With regard to God, a way of indicating his infinite excellence and ever-greaterness: God is so much more than this or that.
Via Negationis (Latin)	The way of negation. The method by which something is denied of a thing. With regard to God, denying of him certain characteristics of finite things: God is not this or that.